book as a life guide as I navigate various challenges of my multicultural lifestyle and I can't wait to see what KC does next! This book is a must read. Thank you KC!"

– Neha O'Rourke, Founder, Career & Energy Coach at Somewhere in Between Coaching LLC

"KC provides a thorough overview, as well as valuable tactics and mindset shifts, for navigating the unique challenges faced by intercultural couples (or their family members). She consistently draws attention to the single most important element of appropriate and effective cross-cultural engagement: our own self-awareness. Drawing on personal experiences, KC leads the reader through critical lessons and skills in cultivating or supporting a successful intercultural relationship. If you're in need of a friend, ally, or guide as you sail these uncharted seas, then you need to read this book."

– Lena Papadopoulos, Interculturalist and Transformation Coach

"KC does a beautiful job to share all the small nuances of intercultural relationships in Loving Across Borders. A mix of guidance and KC's story, her book captures all of the details (big and small) of loving someone who's from a different culture, learning about yourself, setting boundaries, and self-awareness. While reading I finally felt seen, heard, and understood from someone who is in a similar situation as my own. If you find yourself loving someone from a different culture or country, KC and her expertise in this area are like a warm comfort to know you're never alone in this!"

– Cassandra Le, Founder of The Quirky Pineapple Studio

"If you are thinking of marrying someone from another culture, are already in a cross-cultural relationship or have a friend or family member doing so, this book should be required reading. An insightful look at the joys and challenges of intercultural relationships, from one who has been there."

– *Mariam Ottimofiore, Author of 'This Messy Mobile Life' & Blogger at 'And Then We Moved To'*

"This book is the go-to guide to multicultural relationships! KC sensitively and skillfully provides a roadmap on how to navigate common challenges cross-border couples encounter. Whether you've recently fallen in love or have been in a committed relationship for a long time, Loving Across Borders will be a valuable resource – for you, your partner and the closest people around you!"

– *Camilla Quintana, Cert. Life & Relationship Coach for Expat Women*

"This book brought me to tears in a way I've never cried before. It wasn't just KC's beautiful writing, the witty jokes or the actionable tips she gives, but for the way this book is pioneering the unspoken. As a first generation American in an intercultural marriage, this was one of the first times I've felt TRULY seen. KC skillfully makes the reader feel as though she's talking directly to your soul – unraveling the challenges you've had, taking your insecurities head on and celebrating the amazing things about intercultural relationships. KC is so dedicated to her mission and this book is just one of many expressions of that. I can't wait to refer to this

Loving Across Borders

LOVING ACROSS BORDERS

How to Navigate Conflict, Communication, and Cultural
Differences in Your Intercultural Relationship

KC McCormick Çiftçi

Borderless Stories
Chelsea, MI

ISBN 978-1-7344940-0-6 (hardcover)
ISBN 978-1-7344940-1-3 (ebook)

Published by Borderless Stories

www.borderlessstories.com

DEDICATION

For Hüseyin, naturally.

CONTENTS

1

INTRODUCTION

Who Should Read This Book

This book is for you if you've known the joy (and sometimes challenge) of loving someone from another country or culture. If you've ever felt that the people you usually confide in just won't understand you because they don't know how different your reality is from theirs, then it's for you. If you never expected to fall for anyone but the boy/girl next door and then you came home from a trip or a year abroad with more than you bargained for, then it's for you, too. If you're single and dreaming of finding an exotic partner to sweep you off your feet, then it's for you too (but we're going to talk about your use of the word "exotic"). I believe the more realistic we are about the challenges of our relationships, especially in the safe space of being able to share them and be honest about them, the better our chances of growth and success are.

This book is also for the family and loved ones of a person in an intercultural relationship. If you're reading this and this book was a gift from your child or you found it yourself while looking for resources to help you navigate life with a son- or daughter-in-law from another culture, then you are welcome here, too. I honor the work that you are doing to help ease your child into his or her new life and I invite you into the conversation that we are having here. Many of these chapters will help you be more aware of what your child is thinking and feeling, though in Chapter 2 you'll find a section written specifically for you, the family and friends of the people I serve. While you could skip ahead and start there, I don't think reading any of the preceding sections will be a waste of your time.

My Hope for You

It is my sincere hope that this book will help you feel supported, as if you're talking with a close friend. I hope you will read the words on these pages and think, "Oh my gosh, me too! I feel that way, but I just couldn't put it into words!" I especially hope for those moments when you'll think, "I thought I was the only one." My goal and hope in writing this book is to share my inner world in a way that lets you know you can do the same. Not everyone deserves your vulnerability, and you don't owe your story to anyone, but I hope that this book and the community attached to it will connect you with the resources and support that you need.

My Story

Because this may very well be the first time you and I are meeting, let me start with my story and why I am writing this book in the first place, which begs an answer to the question of why Borderless Stories, my company and the publisher of this book, exists at all.

I am a member of the generation that thought travel was the best way to find ourselves, and I was privileged enough to be able to do it. I am an English teacher, or rather, I became an English teacher once I realized that it would be one of the easiest ways for me to find work abroad. The first time I moved to another country, I packed up my suitcase and headed to Ireland for a year to work as a full-time volunteer in a homeless shelter. One of the most commonly asked questions before I left for that trip was, "What are you going to do once this year is up?" And my naïve 23-year-old self wisely knew the answer: "I have no idea. This year is going to change everything."

And that it did. That one year in Ireland led into one year in Germany as a freelance English teacher, which led into one year in South Korea teaching elementary and middle school English while working on my Master's degree at the same time. The combination of experience and my brand new MA allowed me to get a job teaching at a university in Turkey, which is where the real story begins.

First off, I have to say that even the decision to go to Turkey was slightly magical. As my contract in Korea was winding down, I was thinking a lot about what to do next. After being away from home for a few years, coming home in between jobs for a few months before taking off again, I was feeling the pull of growing nieces and nephews, aging grandparents, and relationships defined by Skype rather than hugs and quality time. I was comfortable with the thought of taking a job in the Midwest and spending a few years closer to home, renting an apartment where I could buy or build a bookshelf, rather than living out of a suitcase. While I was working to make this new dream a reality, the posting for a job in Antalya, Turkey crossed my radar, and I felt a stirring that I'd never experienced with any of my previous jobs. On a subconscious level, I knew that that was where I was going next. Turkey had never interested me before, I knew almost nothing about the country, but nevertheless the idea planted itself in my mind and heart from one moment to the next. I applied for the job, interviewed for it at a professional conference where I also interviewed for several Midwestern universities, and ultimately moved to Turkey where a one-year contract became three transformational years.

Friends and family members had always joked with me that "maybe I would meet a nice man this time" as I headed off to a new country. I scoffed and rolled my eyes every time, making it clear that that was NOT what I was looking for. Turkey was no exception.

I met Hüseyin (spoiler alert: we're married now) on my first day of work, which was also his first day of work. But don't worry, this isn't the part of the story where I say it was love at first sight and "when you know, you know." I thought he was cute and struggled to pronounce his name correctly, and we became friendly coworkers and nothing more. I loved the first year at that job; I made great friends, I enjoyed my classes, and the city was the most beautiful place I've ever lived. I renewed my contract for another year, and it was only after making that decision that something shifted and Hüseyin and I saw each other in a new light and began to figure out this whole relationship thing.

We were each other's first boyfriend and girlfriend, which may be surprising if you've done the math and figured out our respective ages at the time. Regardless, that isn't the point of this book or of any of the resources I share. I am not anti-dating, and neither one of us believes that you should only date or be intimate with one person or else you're a sinner; that's just how it happened for us. We both spent enough time alone to figure out a lot of things about ourselves, and could enter our relationship from a starting point of some maturity, along with our inexperience.

As we later moved in together and explored our future, we found ourselves confronting cultural differences in both expected and unexpected places. Some days it felt like everything was an issue; some days we understood each other perfectly. I'd always enjoyed talking things through with my close friends and my mom, but there were arguments that we'd have at times I didn't want to share for fear that no one would be able to relate to me and I'd feel judged. I found myself wishing for resources, a community that understood me, and the support that comes along with that community. I spent a lot of time searching for just that, and when I couldn't find it, I decided to create it.

Thus, Borderless Stories was born. What started with sporadic blogging now incorporates a podcast, coaching services, a vibrant community, this book, and a whole list of ideas for future growth. I guess I heard one too many motivational speakers talk about "being who you needed when you were younger," and at some point it was enough to make me take the plunge.

What gives meaning to my work is hearing the relief in a woman's voice when I say, "I understand, and I've been there." Seeing couples thrive, both together and as individuals reminds me I'm on the right track. Hearing the joy and excitement from someone who has invested in herself and her relationship and seen it pay dividends gives me joy and excitement, too. While writing this book, I brain dumped the following into my journal, and I hope it helps convey why we do what we do:

> "I am grateful for the impact [Borderless Stories] has, which is what drives me to do it every day. On an individual level, I know the importance of support, community, and personal development well. But it goes beyond that. As we transform ourselves, we transform our relationships, and that can break generational patterns and redefine the DNA of our societies and generations to come. As we bump up against people from different countries and cultures than our own, we are confronted by how similar we all are, and it becomes harder and harder to 'other' people. It's the hope we have for peace and understanding in the future – that where there has been ignorance or hatred, there can now be a crack for the light to get in. So that, for example, where we've been, God forgive us, indifferent to the suffering of others, potentially imposed by our own governments, instead we'll have a personal connection, because that's where caring starts. And it spreads from there. I love to hear someone say, 'I want to go to [country they've never previously felt an interest in]. My [obscure connection]'s husband/ wife/partner is from there, and it seems like a cool place.' May we be ambassadors for our shared

humanity, that which connects and unites across borders of all kinds."

Disclaimer

It's important to me we start off with the disclaimer that it's not hard to love someone from a different country or culture. While I often use the language of "unique challenges" in this book and throughout my larger body of work, I want to be clear: I don't think the unique challenges of intercultural life are that people from other countries or different cultures than ours are difficult to love or that it's challenging to be in relationship with them. So, if there's someone in your life who's treating you like you should have a badge of honor because it's so difficult to love someone from another country, honestly, you don't need that kind of talk in your life. Instead, I would say that love is the kind of thing that is simple but not easy. I wouldn't say that it's hard to love anyone, but it requires work and it is something that doesn't just happen on its own without intention and effort. It's something that you need to choose to do over and over again.

So, when we talk about unique challenges that happen in intercultural relationships, we're talking predominantly about legal issues like immigration, communication issues like multiple languages, and cultural challenges that don't come from one culture being superior to another or inferior to another, but just from being influenced by different value systems. Being in an intimate relationship is a choice that you make and there are a lot of questions that come up, and things that we have to figure out ourselves that a lot of other couples don't face. We have to answer questions like, "Where are we going to live?" or, "Is one of us going to be okay with living far away from their country for a lifetime or are we going to be splitting our time or are we going to live in one place for a while and then move to the other?" We ask, "What happens if something calls us to the other country before we're ready, whether it's aging parents, a political situation, or a career opportunity? Are we both open to that possibility?"

In addition to the challenges that anyone can face in a relationship, like how to communicate well or how to show love and respect in the way that the other person receives it best, we also have the challenges of differences in our cultural systems and value systems. The reality is that anyone can be in an intercultural relationship even if they are from the same country, from the same culture, or from the same hometown because our culture is so heavily influenced by family and the way in which we grow up. All of our unconscious value systems, thought patterns, and belief systems are formed during our childhoods and they're not formed consciously and intentionally. They're formed just by observing the world around us and making rules about how it works based on our observations. These can be rules we start to believe about relationships by watching our parents and their relationship with each other, whether it's positive and they communicate well and they seem to respect each other or it's negative or even violent or abusive. This shapes how we see relationships and how we imagine our own relationships unfolding, whether or not we want them to be influenced. We might not want to emulate our parents and yet still have to do a great deal of work to overcome the thought patterns that have cropped up based on who they are.

One truth I believe when it comes to finding a person to be in a relationship with is that you (and I) don't know what you (and I) need. I know there are exceptions to every rule and there are some people who know what they need, but in my experience the only thing I know for sure is that I know nothing. What I mean by this is after years and years of being single, I was often told by people that I needed to create this specific idea of who my dream partner would be and write it down like a shopping list. I heard this from members of a faith community that I was a part of, and I've heard it from people in other communities and in different ways since then. For example, when people talk about manifesting the future that you want, there's an idea that you can "order" your ideal person from God or the universe based on your preferred specifications.

Today, when I look back on what that list would have included at any point in time, it's clear that I had no idea what I needed. I am thrilled to be in the relationship that I am in, but at no time would I have written just the right things down on that list to call this person into my life. I wouldn't say I believe there's only one person who we can make a life with. I think it's a choice and when two people choose to make it work, then that's the whole point. I don't think my younger self would have known to ask for the deep things that really matter. I think I would have been distracted by surface level requests and I know I would have really missed out.

I write this as encouragement for anyone who's facing unexpected challenges or doubting their choice because it's not what you imagined it would be. Just because life hasn't met your expectations doesn't mean it's not just right for you.

Along that same line, when you set out to do work on yourself or your relationship and create the future that you want, it's important to remember what you have ownership over. Spoiler alert: it's only you — your decisions, your actions, your choices. You can invite your partner to be a part of something, but you cannot and should not force him or her to be a part of it. Let me explain what this means to me, day to day. I take some time every day as part of my morning routine to think about goals I have for myself for the future. And when I write or say these statements, I always keep it in the first person singular. I always say, "I am going to do this" or, in more affirmation-specific language, I say, "I have already done this." Even though I've talked with my husband often enough to know that our goals for the future are aligned, it doesn't feel right to me to pull him along on something that I want to create. I share these statements with him, and I let him know what I'm working on or what I'm aiming towards, even sharing how my routine works. But by not expecting him to take part in that or use the same routine as me, it's only me I can be frustrated with or disappointed in for not meeting that goal.

That's not to say I believe in beating myself up for not meeting my goals either, but I think it's a lot easier to be hard on the person we're closest to when they don't meet expectations we have set for them. So, it seems unnecessary to me to set additional specific expectations about the person I hope my husband will be in the future. I think it's fine to have hopes and plans and aims for myself and to trust that they're aligned, but not to be the partner who's dragging the other one along, kicking and screaming. I think the same can be true for many decisions we make together, whether that's about getting married in the first place or having children or where you want to live, what you want your career to look like, or what kind of work you want to do on your relationship.

Having conversations is imperative. Being on the same page is too, but expecting or demanding or giving your power to someone else by saying, "If you do this thing, I'll be happy and fulfilled and if you don't do this thing, I won't be and our relationship will be bad too," is just unfair.

With all of that thoroughly disclaimed, let's dive into what you came here to read. The following chapters are arranged into topics that may be sources of stress or conflict, so you are certainly welcome to hop around as you feel moved. Of course, you won't miss out on anything by reading it through from top to tail, either.

2

YOU'RE NOT
ALONE

The Road Can Be Lonely, But You Aren't Alone

The purpose of this book (and of all the work we do at Borderless Stories) is first and foremost to reassure you that you are not alone. I know from experience that the early stages of an intercultural relationship (and okay, sure, not just the early stages) can make you feel so totally alone. When you and your partner have an argument based on a misunderstanding, you feel like you can't confide in the people you'd normally talk to because they just won't understand. When you're navigating the tricky topics we'll outline in this book, such as cultural expectations for gender roles, religion, or child rearing, it can be really difficult for people who aren't in the same position to relate. If you tell your best friend that your partner believes you should stay home with your future children, for example, your friend may feel disgusted and say, "Ugh. I thought he was better than that. Turns out he's just a sexist pig." But because your friend isn't in the same situation, she doesn't have the full story, right? Her feelings might be more valid if she were thinking of someone born and raised in the same environment as the two of you, but approaching different cultural values with such a black and white, right and wrong mentality only breeds judgment — judgment first and foremost of the other culture for being "wrong" and then ultimately judgment of you, too, for not being "smart" enough to avoid getting yourself in that situation in the first place.

So yes, if you bite your tongue around your loved ones and fear honestly sharing your life with them, I understand and I've been there. We like to paint with broad brushes — we think we know what is good and bad and we think we should all already know those things. We don't leave room for learning, evolving, or open discussion. We'd rather write off our friends' "shitty" foreign boyfriends and girlfriends and by extension their whole country, culture, or religion. What's hilarious about this is that we are ready to dismiss people for not being open-minded enough or tolerant enough, and then our solution is to shut them out and demonize them, which seems pretty close-minded and intolerant to me.

I've heard the relief in my clients' voices when they've dared to share an honest struggle with me. I open our sessions by talking about the importance of being able to talk about what's going on without fear of judgment and dismissal. It often feels like they are gingerly testing the waters when they share a recent struggle, whether it be with housework, sex, religion, politics, security, money, immigration, or anything else in between. I feel them almost holding their breath, wondering what I'm going to say. And when I say, "I get it" or "I've been there" or "There's nothing wrong with you for feeling that way," I feel the relief sigh right out of them. We all know this, right? It feels so good to be seen and understood and told there's nothing wrong with you or with your experience. In fact, there are others just like you going through the same things — what a relief!

...But Marriage Is a Practical Decision

One area where couples with different nationalities experience judgment aplenty is marriage — specifically, the decision to get married in the first place. Eyebrows raise when you share your engagement, where you may have been expecting champagne and congratulations. People question why he or she would want to marry you and if they might just be after your citizenship. Nothing makes you feel so loved or supported as hearing that the one you love doesn't love you for your sense of humor or caring heart but for your friggin' passport, right?

The truth is that marriage is always a practical decision. No matter how romantic comedies or love songs spin it, no one enters into a marriage without at least once thinking about if this is or isn't a good idea and how it will work logistically. If you're from the same country, you might not have quite the same intense discussions, but you'll at least think about if you have the same desires around having children or practicing a religion or moving to a new state. And if you don't already live together, then you'll definitely need to discuss that and figure out where to live. The odds are good you won't continue to live on your own and just meet up once a week.

So, I sure wish we would stop shaming intercultural couples for the practical conversations that they have or making them pretend that those aren't a part of their reality. You don't accidentally end up married to someone and successfully immigrating, and the way it works is to get on the same page and get serious about paperwork. Now, that's not romantic or sexy, but it sure as hell is important. If someone says that part of the reason they got married is so that they could continue to be together in the same country, that is not a judgment-worthy statement. If a couple decides to commit more quickly than you think they should because one of them is about to have to leave the country, you're missing the most important part of that statement: they are a COUPLE. Two people in a romantic relationship (neither one of which is you). The decision is theirs, and if their relationship already existed prior to this decision, there's no need to run through the streets screaming that it's a green card marriage. In its most classic meaning, a green card marriage is not based on an existing romantic relationship but simply a contract between two people that benefits one of them in terms of immigration (and no, I do not condone this). If your friend is telling you that she is engaged to her boyfriend who happens to be from a faraway place, that's not the same thing. Imagine how you would feel if that same friend questioned your relationship: maybe your partner is just with you for your superior health insurance, sweet apartment, or great genes for future progeny.

Share This with Your Family and Friends

Following is an adaptation of a blog that I wrote in early 2019. It's a piece that I wrote with the intention that it might raise awareness and spare our community members from awkward and uncomfortable moments. I took the challenges and frustrations I had experienced and observed with family and friends of a person with a non-citizen partner. It may be helpful for you to share this with people in your life, either by passing on this book when you're finished, snapping a picture of these pages, or finding the original blog online.

The piece is titled "Advice for American In-Laws," and before anyone asks, no, this advice isn't unique to Americans. I think anyone with a son- or daughter-in-law from another country would benefit from reading it, but I feel more comfortable addressing it to Americans. This is done in the spirit of "calling in" people from my own country, rather than speaking like I'm criticizing a group of which I'm not a member.

Open your mind

It is hard for all of us to have our world views challenged. Creatures of habit, we definitely are. But if you've been blessed with a brand new son- or daughter-in-law from a country different than your own, you've just gotten such a beautiful opportunity to have your view expanded. And this is passive education — you don't even need to crack open a book if you don't want to!

If you've got some preconceived notions about the country where your child's partner is from, I challenge you to let them go. Maybe the first time you heard about this new special someone, you felt a twinge in your stomach. You may be worried that he's a playboy or she's a gold digger based solely on hearing where he or she is from. I know parents never stop worrying about their kids, but I do hope you didn't share these exact concerns with your child while they were excitedly telling you their news. If so, it's entirely possible they're going to be a bit defensive, but that doesn't mean your relationship is damaged irreparably.

Be prepared to get to know your son or daughter's person as a person, not only as a member of his or her religion, citizen of his or her country, or based on any other label. You may be pleasantly surprised that the things that unite us are far greater than the things that divide us.

Ask questions

A great way to get to know a new member of your family is to ask questions. Especially if this new member of your family is feeling a bit shy, gently including him or her in shared activities and taking an interest in him or her as a person will go a long way to building your relationship.

You may want to ask questions about his or her country or religion, too (among other things). This is going to vary from person to person, but the best rule to follow is to be respectful and not make assumptions. If you have an idea about the region of the world where he or she is from, this may not be the time to share it. If, for example, you find yourself wanting to say, "Africa/ The Middle East/Asia is so _____," I'd encourage you to hit the "pause" button on that. Has anyone ever made a blanket statement about the USA to you? How did you feel? Were you defensive, ready to prove them wrong? Or did it invite you into further conversation? In that situation, I've found myself explaining that the USA is a big country and that therefore there is nothing universally true about every region, state, or citizen. I recommend that we apply this same logic to generalizations about regions of the world. At the time of publication, Africa has a population over 1.2 billion, the Middle East contains around 60 languages, and Asia is made up of 48 countries. Those numbers are vast, and certainly don't incline me to want to make generalizations about all of the people they include.

Instead of sharing our opinions about regions or countries where we haven't been (or may have spent a limited amount of time), I recommend asking questions. You've got an expert in your midst, so why not be a willing student at his or her feet. Avoid leading questions or ones that show prejudice, but open-ended questions can be a great way to learn. *What was your childhood like? What are your favorite holiday traditions? What are some folk tales in your country? Are there any sports in your country that I may not have heard of?* You've got a living, breathing expert in a new country in your family, so I'm sure you can think of some interesting questions to ask. At the same time, it is important to remember that a question does not demand an answer — it is an invitation to share, and the choice falls to the one being asked if he or she would care to answer. Remember that you are not entitled to any parts of someone's story that he or she does not want to share.

Respect differences

Try to remember that different does not mean wrong. There are such a range of things you may discover differing between you that it's almost impossible to even issue a warning. You may have wildly different opinions on politics, capitalism, celebrations, the cure for the common cold, fashion, and any and everything in between. Regardless, the best way to navigate this is going to be with curiosity and not judgment. This new son- or daughter-in-law may celebrate different holidays or the same ones with different traditions. The food he or she cooks may not taste like anything you've ever eaten before. He or she may have a different level of comfort with physical contact and affection. He or she may dress more conservatively or provocatively than you're used to. None of this is wrong, and if you can both respect each other, it'll be the greatest wedding gift (even belated) that you can give your child.

Be mindful of language

This may not seem like as big a deal as the others mentioned, but what can I say — I'm a language teacher, so I can't just leave out this pet peeve of mine. Language can be isolating or including, and it's entirely up to the ones who hold the power. In this case, that would be those who can fluently speak the language that most interaction is taking place in. If you've spoken English since birth and your child's spouse is not a native speaker of English, then there may be a level of difficulty that you aren't aware of. As you interact with him or her, try to become more aware of the way that you speak. Are you using a lot of idioms that he or she probably didn't learn in school? Are you referencing pop culture that he or she might not know? Are you making lots of inside jokes?

In the classroom, I always adapt my speech to the level of my students. With my most basic students, I cut out idioms entirely and try to stick to the present tense. With more advanced students, I increase my speed and let a little more difficult vocabulary and grammar find its way into my speech. It's work, yes, and I often feel relieved at the end of a day of teaching when I can relax with my loved ones and speak freely. I'm not suggesting that you adopt the exact same principles here, but being more aware of your speech will help your new family member feel more included. Try to use fewer quotes from 90s sitcoms, outdated idioms, and work to find the parts of humor that are universal.

3

SELF-AWARENESS

One of the most important skills we can develop is self awareness. I think it's incredibly important for our own growth to be aware of ourselves, and there's no place where this is more true than in our relationships, so this is something we really all need to consider. No matter who our relationship is with, and even if you're single, there are so many benefits to developing self-awareness. Now, if you've made it this far in the book and aren't actually in an intercultural relationship, I guarantee this is the most useful chapter to you and to anyone. It's something that we will all benefit from in every relationship in our lives, whether it's personal, professional, or a friendship.It will benefit from us becoming more aware of ourselves, the way that we show up in the world, the way that we communicate with others, and the way that we express ourselves. It's a beautiful, wonderful thing, and there's so much to be learned on this journey into yourself.

So first and foremost, let's talk about our partners as mirrors. This is a concept that I've learned from my husband, though I know he didn't make it up. But it's a fascinating thing, the way that we mirror each other and the way that when one of us has an issue with the other, that tends to end up being about the first person. Now that might be confusing the way that I said that, so let me explain it in a different way. Think about a friend or a colleague or someone that you know who is always complaining to you about a different person in their life.

So let's think about roommates. Someone comes to you who has a new roommate, and after a couple of weeks they say it's not working out for some reason. "That roommate did/didn't _____. I just can't live with them." Then they get a new roommate and a few weeks after that, sure enough, they're telling you, "Well, that one didn't work out either. I can't live with that person because of this reason and that reason." I have witnessed this in my own life where someone complains about roommate after roommate as they continue to change roommates and then at some point, that person is looking for roommates again and asking you for a suggestion. If you're anything like me, you'll say, "No, I don't know of anyone who needs a roommate," even though you may very well know someone because what you start to realize is that this person is always having a problem with their roommates and you can't help but question, well, what's the common denominator here?

Has this always been about the other people or is there something about it that's really about you? Honestly, I think the same thing is true with relationships. That's not to say that we could make it work with absolutely anyone that we're in a relationship with. There are certainly exceptions and I would never ever condone someone staying in a relationship that is abusive or manipulative. But there are things that come up as a pattern in a relationship where if we continue to leave and to go and find someone new, there are aspects of ourselves that we won't explore likely because they're too uncomfortable. So what I've learned in a close intimate relationship is that if there's something about me that bothers my husband, it's usually really about him and if there's something about him that bothers me, it's really usually about me.

You know, there's a quote that says we hate the most in others what we despise in ourselves. And I wouldn't exactly apply that here because I don't think that using the word "hate" really should apply to our closest relationships. But the truth is that there are things that we see in other people that drive us nuts and it would be really helpful to look at ourselves and say, "Hmm, do I ever do that? Is there a reason that that bothers me and is it about me? Is it about something that I do and the way that I am existing in this world?"

For example, something that has been challenging for me with my husband at a brief time in our relationship was seeing the ways that he was growing, especially spiritually, and feeling scared of being left behind and kind of lashing out at him in some ways and saying, "Why are you doing this? You shouldn't do this," or trying to talk him out of it. And then realizing that this was really about my own fear and at the same time that his growth was difficult for me to accept, I expected him to accept my growth. So there were plenty of things that I had gone through in that time and ways that I had changed and when it had been hard for him to see me change, I was kind of like, "Well get on board with it, Mister. This is happening," but then not returning that favor when the shoe was on the other foot. So it's an interesting phenomenon how that works, but the answer, the only way that we've found peace in that is by having honest conversation with each other about these things and by saying, "Wow, now I understand how you feel because I'm doing the same thing back at you."

It's a very special thing to have someone in your life who is a mirror and who you can be a mirror to and to treat that as an honor. And it's an opportunity to learn and to grow together. One thing I like to say is we shouldn't enter into a relationship expecting another person to change, of course not. But we also should be prepared to continue to love them when they do change because the reality is this intense kind of growth that we go through by being together is going to spark change, is going to to spur us along on our journey of personal growth. And we don't want to be the ones who are looking at our partner and saying, "Hmm, you were different when I met you, so I'm not sure about this." Of course there are times when that is going to be the sad reality that we've changed too much and it doesn't work. But just because something is a little scary or a little unfamiliar, it doesn't mean that we have to wish things back to the way that they were. So for me, that's my husband's spiritual growth, and I can't wish that he hadn't gone on that journey. And at the same time, as I've become more of an entrepreneur, putting myself out there more in the world, I don't want him to try to make me smaller and he doesn't want to try to make me smaller either.

Relationships, as it might be clear here, are a great opportunity to learn about yourself. I think the best possible way to learn how to communicate with another person is actually first to learn about yourself. Because if you don't understand who you are and why you are the way you are, then it's really, really hard to understand that other person. So I like to use the metaphor, it's the same image of an iceberg that we see when we look at culture, with the visible up above the surface and the much larger invisible part underneath the surface. So the same thing exists within an individual. So there are all these parts of ourselves that you can see, and we think often that they are the most important, most significant parts of ourselves, the way that we dress, the way that we style our hair, the way we look, the behaviors that we have, without realizing that those deep unconscious things that we have absorbed from the world around us, no one has taught them to us, those beliefs and thought patterns and values, those really influence who we are, how we interact with others, and how we interact with the world around us.

4

THINGS TO
TALK ABOUT
BEFORE
GETTING
MARRIED

Know Your Deal-Breakers

The process of starting a life with your intercultural love is not one to enter into lightly. As we begin this in-depth exploration of all the considerations to keep in mind, it is important to be aware of the spaces where you are not willing to compromise. This can mean many different things to different people: maybe you will not consider raising your child in a religion different than your own, or maybe you have no interest in living in your partner's home country. Even reading those sentences, you may feel some resistance, like, "What kind of jerk wouldn't even consider that? Rude!" but if these thoughts and feelings are swirling in your mind and/or heart, refusing to acknowledge them isn't going to make them go away. Let this be a judgment-free space. Maybe at this point in your life you cannot imagine compromising on the above issues. Start by admitting to yourself that those topics are not on the table for discussion with you. It isn't fair to your partner to lead him or her to believe that you are open to something that you aren't. If you both feel very strongly that your children should be raised in your religion of birth and those religions are different, then there is a very important conversation that needs to be had. Likewise, if you want to retire in your home country and your partner can't imagine being away from the place he or she knows and loves, then you need to discuss that as well.

You may not realize how strongly you feel about any particular topic like this, and it is my hope that this book can serve as a conversation starter to see if you both, in fact, are on the same page. I caution you not to hold out a lot of hope for your future together if your "deal-breaker" list is as long as a CVS receipt. The nature of intimate relationship success is compromise, so taking a "my way or the highway" attitude about a multitude of things is likely not going to start you off on the right foot. However, if there are one or two things that are of vital importance to you, you may be able to work with that. Be willing to compromise in other areas, and be open to solutions that you will both appreciate. For example, if you feel you must live in your homeland, then at the very least, have a plan for how many visits you will make to your partner's family and how much time you will spend with them in a year.

The Need for Intention

In American culture, it doesn't seem that uncommon for young folks to just kind of slide into marriage as the next step of their journey together. With the divorce rate hovering around 50%, it suggests that this isn't a decision universally entered into with great care and concern, and the reality of the global divorce rate suggests that the rest of the world doesn't think that much differently.

I am not here to write a diatribe about divorce by any means. I have seen relationships where divorce truly was the best option for both members, as well as abusive relationships where divorce may have saved a life. Marriages that end in divorce cannot universally be classified as failures — some relationships are seasonal, and the end does not nullify the experience.

With that disclaimer, let me say that divorce can be seen as an easy option when people stop having the same easy, warm-fuzzy feelings about their partner, and that is a luxury that many intercultural couples cannot afford. While the natural progression of a relationship between two high school sweethearts may be dating, engagement, and a beautiful wedding as markers of the passage of time, couples separated by an ocean or two need to be intentional about what their future together holds.

[I should add another disclaimer. If you are as rich as God, this probably doesn't apply to you as much. If you can afford to see each other as much as you want, then you may not feel the same pressure that average

Joe does. Of course, I don't know what the odds are that you are even reading this book, but it's worth noting nonetheless.]

Most of us in the international/intercultural relationship space aren't in a position to just let life happen to us. It's likely that if we don't have some major conversations, we will be separated by miles and time zones and expensive flights. While my husband and I entered into our relationship with the motto, "We'll see what happens," when the time came to figure out our next steps, it didn't work quite the same way.

Immigration is not for the faint of heart, much to the dismay of pop culture where movies and TV shows depict the relative ease that couples have when entering into a marital commitment. For the average person, the fiance or spousal visa process is expensive, long, and emotionally taxing. What begins with a 10-page application ends with a file detailing your whole lives together being sent to an immigration officer to dissect. It is not something that you do just for the heck of it, to see if they'll accept you, the way you might apply to a university that probably won't like your SAT scores. It is a process that is entered into with great hope that it will succeed, though you should have a Plan B in mind in case it doesn't.

Trust Your Heart, and Use Your Brain

The idea of "trusting your heart" is so romantic, don't you think? That organ that beats in your chest, keeping you alive can also detect its soulmate from across a crowded room. While I absolutely do not believe that the human heart is incapable of making a mistake, I do allow the need to trust and follow it in matters of romance and partnership. Despite all the bureaucracy of the immigration process (or perhaps because of it), it is important to keep your heart engaged in the process so you remember why in the world you began this journey of stress and separation in the first place.

There is an amount of trusting yourself, whether that is your heart, your intuition, or your gut, that needs to happen to get any relationship off the ground. If every fiber of your being is screaming, "NO!" at you, it's unlikely that your relationship will make it far. By that same token, though, it's important that your brain is engaged in the process too.

If you love someone dearly, you may be willing to overlook any number of red flags. This is where your brain would serve you well. If your heart says, "Go!" but your brain says, "Well, what about her addiction?" or "What about the time he was unfaithful?" then you need to listen up. The belief that love is enough won't get you far when these issues rear their ugly heads. This is true and important in any relationship, but I mention it here because I believe it is even more important in an intercultural one.

Let me give an example. If you and your partner move heaven and earth to be together and finally manage to be reunited with both of you having legal status in the same country, that is something to celebrate. But what if before this whole process began you had an argument that got physically violent? You may tell yourselves it was due to extenuating circumstances — the stress of immigration or a one-time misunderstanding. It is easy enough to put someone's negative traits out of your mind when you are separated and longing for each other's company.

Absence makes the heart grow fonder, and all that jazz. But if and when the separation ends and you are reunited, whatever that little problem was before, it will come too. Your partner may think he or she is leaving that problem behind in their home country, but little problems always find a way to stow away in your suitcase, and once they cross an ocean or two they can become even bigger problems. If you thought your partner was stressed before, just imagine what adding culture shock, homesickness, wedding planning, and unemployment to the mix will do. I do not say this to scare you, but to caution you. Whatever you are willing to overlook now can not possibly be overlooked forever. Problems do not go away by sticking your head in the sand, rest assured.

None of this is shared with the intention of scaring you away from love and risk. There are no guarantees in life, and love and commitment always involves risk. At the chance that there's no one else in your life to do it, I'm here to provide a "both/and" perspective. Maybe the only skepticism you've heard is from people questioning the very nature of your relationship and doing it in a way that feels gross and judgmental. Well, I both believe your relationship is real and I want you to use your wits and senses before leaping into a commitment.

5

CULTURE & CONFLICT

The DIVE Framework

In this chapter we'll talk about navigating conflict, and I'd like to be clear that this technique does not apply only to romantic relationships and it does not apply only to intercultural relationships. In all honesty, any relationship can be intercultural since culture is so strongly shaped by your family of origin, and basically, if you're dealing with anyone who's not in your family (and sometimes even people who are in your family), you're dealing with a different culture.

So without further ado, we are going to dive in, and we're going to talk about culture, communication, and conflict and how the heck to navigate them in a graceful way. You have likely seen the illustration before of culture as an iceberg — it's been around since 1976, when Edward T. Hall first introduced it to us. So either from that, from the movie "Titanic" or from National Geographic, I'm guessing you know what an iceberg looks like. There's a smaller amount up above the surface, and then there's this large, large, large part underneath the surface. We often have culture explained to us with this image because of the two components. The top part, the visible part, is your behavior. These are parts of culture, like drinking tea regularly, the clothes that you wear, customs, or anything else that we can see. These things make us say, "Oh, that's an interesting culture, look at that dance that they're doing. Look at the fact that they sit on the floor or sit on chairs, or use chopsticks or use forks or use their hands to eat."

Next is the middle section, which is both above the waterline and below it. This is belief. Sometimes parts of our beliefs are visible, if for example, we dress in a certain way because of our religious or cultural beliefs. But there is also a significant portion of our beliefs that are invisible things that we don't share, things that we might not even be aware of ourselves.

Finally, down in the depth, way at the bottom of the iceberg, you have values and thought patterns that are deeply ingrained by our culture. This includes things that we see as normal in pop culture, that perhaps someone else might not see as normal. It's often hard to explain how this part of the iceberg influences us, or even to be aware of it. This could be values about gender roles, family obligations, responsibilities, and expectations, to name just a few.

What I am suggesting here is that the same model of an iceberg works for an individual, and especially an individual who is in a relationship with another person. I have my own iceberg. I have things that are visible about me: you can see the way I dress, you can see the way I speak, you can see the books I read, you can see the music I listen to, and plenty more. But then there are also things that you can't see and that even I can't see. I might not be aware of my beliefs, my values, my thought patterns, or why I respond the way that I do to different things that happen. The same thing is true for any other person that I interact with. For an example, I think about my husband, because that's my closest relationship. He also has plenty of aspects that I see: I see his behavior, I see the things that he laughs at, I see the things that he is entertained by, I see the food he eats, and so on. But then there's a great deal that I don't see and that he might also be unaware of.

What is interesting about a relationship is that we often think we can see the invisible stuff in the other person. We think we can look at our partner, a family member, or someone we work with, and we can say, "You're like [this] because of [that]. And I know that about you." We might be accurate about this sometimes, but it's so much easier to direct these statements at another person, instead of reflecting on ourselves and saying, "Well, hold on a second, what about me? What about why I'm reacting the way I'm reacting?" So my suggestion is this: always, always, always look at yourself first. This is the recipe for peace in a relationship. And it's the recipe for change, because the only thing that you can change is yourself and your reactions, and you cannot change another person. They may be inspired by you and your actions, but you cannot change them.

I have a framework that I have come up with to explain how to do the work of reflecting on ourselves to resolve conflict. And before we dive into it, let's remember this: when something happens and the potential for a conflict comes up between you and another person, what we need to do, instead of looking at that other person is to start with ourselves. It is easy to sit comfortably on top of our own iceberg, looking over at our partners and calling, "Hey, I see some funky stuff down below the surface there, you need to clean that up!" Instead of doing that, what we need to do is put on our really warm, insulated wetsuits (metaphorically, of course), and dive down next to our own iceberg, and investigate it. We can poke around and answer our questions. "What's going on here? What's the deal with this thing?" which means, "What's my deal? Why am I feeling the way I'm feeling? Why am I reacting the way I'm reacting? What's going on with me?" Maybe when we're deep down underwater, maybe we'll look over and we see, "Oh, hey, yeah, that person that I love, that I'm doing this life thing with, they're doing the same thing, checking out their own iceberg." And then we can interact. But even if that doesn't happen, at least we're doing the work ourselves so we can understand, so we can progress, and so we can make steps in the right direction to feel more whole and feel more able to navigate a wider range of topics and conflicts.

So, without further ado, here comes the framework. I'm calling it the DIVE framework, because I never met a metaphor about water or icebergs that I didn't love. Now let's walk through all the steps of this, because you might be looking at it right now and thinking it looks pretty wacky. The first two steps say "Detect" and then "Ignore" — how does that make sense? But I promise there's a rhyme and reason to it.

The first step is that you detect a reaction in yourself. These are your Spidey senses. Something tingles, and you suddenly feel that you're about to shout or you're about to get really quiet and give someone the silent treatment or whatever it is you do when you react. Some of us can feel this in our bodies, whether it's a feeling in the pit of your stomach or the sweaty palms of anxiety. So, we notice it. We become aware that something's going on inside us.

Then, step two is to ignore. And no, I don't mean that we should ignore the feeling that we've just detected within ourselves and pretend everything is fine. No, this means that you should ignore your partner — and again, I need to clarify, right? I don't mean that you should stop listening to your partner and give him or her that silent treatment we talked about. I mean that you should ignore the perceived wrongs that you are detecting in this moment from your partner. So it means to ignore that whole bottom part of your partner's iceberg. Instead of climbing up high to get a glimpse of his or her iceberg then casting judgment towards it, remember that that's not your territory. Stay away from it, and put on your blinders, like an old timey horse. Don't even look at what isn't for you to fix or change.

The third step is to dive in, dive way down deep, and investigate. And this is the part where you go full Sherlock Holmes on yourself, and you dig around in your insides. You ask yourself, "Why are you reacting this way? What's making you feel this way? What thoughts are you having? Why are you having these thoughts? What experiences have happened that have made you have these thoughts and therefore feelings and therefore beliefs and recurring beliefs?" There are lots of strategies for doing this kind of work. Sometimes something as simple as journaling can be really powerful because sometimes you don't really know what's going on inside of yourself until you start writing it. There's something about that physical movement and about the speed at which you can do it. It's not as fast as typing, so it's a little slower, it's a little more methodical,and something might come out that will surprise you and help you understand yourself. You might have an "Aha!" moment like, "Ooh, I remember I had that experience when I was a kid, and it's made me have this belief about privacy, or about division of labor in a romantic relationship, or about money..." or whatever it is. You can take your choice of things that people tend to have conflicts about; you have beliefs about the things that you have conflicts about.

After you've thoroughly Sherlock Holmes-ed yourself, you can move on to the fourth and final step. And, by the way, I don't mean after you've finished step three so thoroughly that you've been in counseling for eight years; I mean you've at least taken a minute or two to check in with yourself. After that, then you come back up, and then you can express what you're ready to say to the other person. You make "I" statements, saying, "I feel this way, because I had an experience that made me believe that [fill in the blank] about [whatever you're having conflict about.]" To pick up with previous examples, maybe, "It makes me believe that something shouldn't be shared with our friends," or, "That makes me believe that we have to live on a strict budget," or whatever it is for you. You're keeping this as something that's about you, and you're not saying, "I'm feeling this way because you're a jerk and I don't know why I married you." (Disclaimer: That is never really a great thing to say, if you're hoping to reach a compromise and have a peaceful interaction.) But if you can say, "I feel this way, because I believe this or because I value this or because I think this," then you're going to get a lot further. The image I like to use for this part is that it's like Ariel in "The Little Mermaid," and this is her swimming back up to the surface and showing off what she has found. We might not feel like we have the same kind of treasure to show off, but we can at least say, "Well, hey, I found this thing inside myself. And here it is, maybe we can make some forward progress with that." It's a lot easier to make forward progress in a conflict or navigation with the other person if you're coming from a place of humility and of wanting to grow and wanting to learn.

It's my hope for you that the other person that you're doing this with is also in that same space. But even if they're not, this is an opportunity for you to learn more about yourself. There's great value in learning about yourself, because that helps you interact with others more effectively, whether that's at work, at home, or with your friends. Anything that helps you learn how you move through the world, understand how you perceive the world and how that might be different from other people might help you. This work helps us realize more and more that it's not so much that one way is right and one way is wrong, but it's just that one way feels familiar to us because it's been part of our environment for our whole lives. It's what we've experienced day in and day out, and it shaped everything.

I'll close this section with an example. Something that people might feel very differently about is individual oriented versus family oriented culture. This is a major difference that encompasses a lot of different cultures. In some cultures, people tend to be more individual minded, more independent, more self-focused. And privacy can come along with that. It might mean you don't want to talk about money, politics, religion, or some other topic that feels private to you. Now, in other cultures that may be more family oriented and have a lot more togetherness, this can be a source of conflict, especially for a romantic partnership.

If one of you sees the world in a family-oriented way and one sees it in an individual-oriented way, that's the perfect breeding ground for a problem when you're around your larger family circle. One partner might feel like they aren't cared for because others aren't asking the right questions or spending enough time together. On the other hand, in the opposite family environment the other partner might be feeling desperate to have a minute alone. So this is sometimes where conflict comes up. Let's say you are the individual oriented person and you're immersed in family for two weeks on end. You're starting to detect a reaction because your partner suggests an activity for all of you to do together. And you start to react and you want to lash out and say, "No, I'm sick of this!" How do you think that is going to go? Instead, you can remind yourself that this way of being isn't wrong, it's just different. You ignore the perceived wrong in it, and instead you opt to investigate your own feelings and reactions. You'll find that moment of discovery, where you say, "Ah, ok, I think I know what's going on here. I have a background where things have tended to be more private and more individual oriented. And that's what I'm comfortable with. That's just how I move through the world." So when you come back up from that, you can express yourself and say, "I feel overwhelmed when I don't get much time alone." It's all about the pronouns, and sticking to "I"s rather than "YOU"s. It becomes an invitation to solve this problem together and move forward together.

Gender Roles (Even if You Don't Think This Affects You)

It would be tempting to dismiss the section on gender roles. You may be thinking, "Oh, my partner isn't anything like those backwards people in his culture who think women only belong in the kitchen. I never would have married someone like that." On the other hand, you may have a relationship where you overtly disagree on appropriate gender roles. Whatever the case, it's a vital topic to explore, whether you can read each others' minds or can't see eye-to-eye to save your lives.

To start with, if you believe your views on gender roles

differ greatly from the culture you grew up in, or if the same is true for your partner, that doesn't mean that you should write off the topic completely. You might have years of experience disagreeing with what people around you are saying and you may be countercultural AF. But there are also aspects of these cultural values that can be deeply internalized, which is why the need for awareness is so vital.

My husband is from a very traditional, family-oriented culture, though he is someone who deeply values equality and would never espouse views that women must do all the cooking, cleaning, or childcare. Despite that, we have still had to confront the differences in our cultures' values around gender roles and division of labor. For him, that has meant becoming aware of internalized values that suggest I should be taking better care of him or our home. For me, it has meant becoming aware of my own laziness. While any suggestion that I should do more work around the house was met with fears that I was not being respected or treated as an equal, the reality was that my husband was already doing more than half of the work around the house and I was just being lazy and comfortable with being cared for. While he was afraid of being taken advantage of and I was too, one of us had a much more legit claim on that fear.

With time, we've come to an arrangement where we both take care of different household responsibilities. There's no need to go against what you're naturally inclined to do, if that works for both of you. I do most of the cooking, he does laundry and vacuums, and we share dishwashing responsibilities.

Let's Not Go the Way of the Titanic

This is where those internalized values mentioned previously come from in the first place. Let's revisit the iceberg, and focus on the part under the water where gender roles are. These elements down in the depths are difficult to quantify, and they often manifest themselves as thoughts and feelings that we can't quite explain. For example, this came up in the early stages of my relationship when my husband and I were first dating. He felt discomfort with the way I interacted with some of our male coworkers, being overly smiley and generally a little goofy. It was difficult for him to explain how he was feeling and why he was feeling that way, and since we didn't know better yet at that point, we argued about it quite often. I would insist that I wasn't flirting, but nothing I said or did could change the way he felt. It was only when we both began to explore our own thoughts and feelings that we managed to resolve the issue at hand. We each thought more about what flirtatious behavior looks like to us, which has an origin in our culture and the examples we've seen. To me, flirting wasn't something I'd ever really done, not in the typical American way. I thought of examples from pop culture, of women laughing too hard at bad jokes, finding excuses to touch the object of their affection, and likely speaking or gesturing in very suggestive ways. My husband had a different definition, and knowing only a handful of Americans at the time it was difficult for him to see a clear distinction in how we viewed appropriate male-female interactions.

If we don't put on our diving suits and delve into the depths to explore just how massive the bottom of our own personal iceberg is, all we'll persist in doing is judging our partners for the parts of their culture that we can see. It's natural to believe something is right because we've known it for our whole lives. But if that's where we stop, then intercultural marriage just won't work. If we aren't willing to do the work on ourselves, then at some point our two massive icebergs will have crashed into each other too many times and will slowly drift apart one last time. Stubbornness can be the death of a good relationship, which makes the willingness to do the work the key to success, in my humble opinion. When you notice discomfort in yourself in a conflict, be ready to explore it in yourself before you toss the blame back to your partner. Accepting responsibility for our own feelings will help us approach conflict as whole beings rather than wounded animals looking for someone to hurt.

6

BELIEF SYSTEMS & RELIGION

This is Personal

Often, when religion is raised as a point of contention for intercultural couples, it comes from family members who are afraid of one of the partners losing his or her religion. Naturally, there are times where the concern comes from the partner himself or herself, but for now let's focus on the role of family preference in the conversation about religion.

To begin with, it is important to remember that a marriage is a partnership, meaning that, while other people may be affected by it, it is by and large something that exists between two people who have made a commitment to each other. This should be a great relief to remember when the topic of religion (or honestly anything related to your future together) comes up. Whether you are deciding what religion you would like to practice or which tradition to raise your children in, the key words in this sentence are "you" and "your." I say this not to disrespect anyone's relatives — fears of family members tend to come from the best intentions — but simply to remind that not everything needs to be up for decision by committee vote. Whatever best suits you and your partner is what you should do. The preferences of your individual families can certainly be entertained and even accommodated when appropriate, but jumping through the hoops set up by two different sets of cultural values is exhausting. I'm of the opinion that jumping through hoops is best left to circus animals, and even then I'm not really fond of it.

Once you've decided with your partner that you will have this conversation without asking Mom or Dad for input, you can begin the real work of deciding together what to do. If neither one of you feels strongly about your religious traditions, then you can start to decide if you'd like to practice none, one, or both of them. If one of you is passionate about your religious views and unwilling to consider any outcome but your partner converting and any future children being raised within that religion, then clearly this is a very important conversation to have. You'd best discuss it with your partner before moving too far ahead in your commitment — if you find that this is a deal breaker for you, then it is better to know that sooner than later.

There are many possible solutions, though, apart from separating from your loved one. There are couples who maintain separate religious identities, and their children may be invited to participate in both until they choose for themselves what they would like to believe. There are also couples where one member converts for the sake of having a wedding ceremony together, or so that their children can be recognized within that faith, though that person's level of commitment to the faith may be in name only.

Do not be afraid to get creative. While you've likely been taught that there are very specific rules for how to practice the faith of your childhood, in the new life and family that you are building, you get to make the rules. Find what works for you and brings peace and joy to the ones you love, and don't worry too much about the labels that others want to place on you.

Conversations to Have with Your Families

After establishing with your partner that you are the captains of your own destiny/future, it may be time to clue your families in on your decisions. There are a few conversations that will help establish those boundaries.

First, if it's safe and appropriate for you, you can let your family know where your belief system differs from their own. Be clear in your love and respect for them and for the traditions that they value, but feel free to let them know that you've taken a different path. It can help to establish that it's you choosing this different life/route, and that your partner isn't someone for them to blame for "corrupting" you.

This may be one of the first areas of your life where you've felt the need to establish boundaries. Don't be nervous about it — this experience will serve you well when it comes time to establish more and more boundaries, as we'll discuss in just a few chapters. One necessary ingredient for successful, effective boundaries is helping your loved ones realize that you are an adult and no longer a child. If you continue your relationship with your parents, for example, in the same way that you related to them as a child, it will be difficult for them to see you as an autonomous individual.

There are benefits for everyone involved from creating these boundaries in your family. They will strengthen your relationship with your family, counterintuitive as it may seem. You may fear telling your parents that you're an adult and can make your own decisions, but in a way, doing this will make it easier for them to see you as an adult, a peer, an equal. When they no longer feel responsible for your life, it can free them up to focus on their own interests, dreams, hobbies, and so on.

I realize I'm saying this from the perspective of a fairly individualistic culture and society. However, I've seen this put into effect in more family-oriented cultures as well, with great success. While there is plenty that your culture does determine, there is no need to let it determine your boundaries. Even if it seems completely radical in your country or culture, set limits. You can do it in a loving way to avoid burning bridges or needlessly hurting feelings, but if you opt out of doing it, you may find yourself resenting those same people that you didn't want to hurt. If it is going to negatively impact your relationship — if you are going to grumble and wish that they could read your mind, then it is an act of kindness to everyone involved to create the space that you so desperately crave.

Whether you adhere to a particular set of religious

views or not, there are benefits for both you and any future generations from being exposed to multiple world views. Whichever side of the coin you find yourself on, the truth is that there are many different religions and ways of seeing the world. Learning about them can help you understand the people that you interact with who subscribe to those views. If you are a believer in one particular faith, there's no need to feel challenged by the faiths of others. They can strengthen your own faith, and faith that is easily threatened by hearing about the way someone else thinks or prays may benefit from strengthening. As far as your children go, surely you want them to choose their faith of their own free will rather than being forced into it. If this is the case, then there is no harm in learning about different ways of thinking, approaches to rational and spiritual thought, traditions, and standards for morality. While doing this may convince you that your religion is the one true one and all the others are for morons, my hope is that you'll find a healthy appreciation for the values of others without feeling the need to judge or compare.

For those who are not adherents of one faith, you may find practices and traditions from both your upbringing and your partner's that you'd like to introduce to your children. If you don't want to choose just one, there is no reason not to sample from both of your experiences. People crave to know where they came from — just look at the popularity of DNA kits to tell you where in the world your ancestors lived. Whether they appreciate it now or won't until they're adults, your children want to know about their origins. Introduce them to the holidays you both celebrate, and give them the opportunity to sit with older relatives to hear passed down stories about traditions. Better yet, if you can record those relatives, either in writing or in video form, your family will love to have that history lesson in later years.

"Me" or "We"

Belief systems can be difficult to talk about, so I'll tread lightly here. I know for many of us religion is considered a taboo topic, and plenty of others of us would prefer only to discuss something like this with a member of the clergy or an interfaith practitioner. I understand and respect that, and I'll navigate this in a way that I hope will be helpful without being overly prescriptive.

Rather than focus exclusively on religion, I think it's important to talk about beliefs as a whole, especially since they occupy the mysterious region of the culture iceberg that's both above and below the water line. When it comes specifically to religion, many of us may already have an idea of what works for us in our relationships, whether that's practicing our faith together, keeping it personal, or blending our unique traditions. But for those in the earlier stages of an intercultural relationship, you may still be trying to figure out what your deal breakers are. "Am I trying to get you to kind of come over to my side of things? Are we trying to compromise and meet in the middle? How is this working?"

Whether we're talking about faith, dietary choices like vegetarianism, or anything else that's based on a belief, you have to ask yourself exactly one question. Is it a "me" thing or is it a "we" thing? That's the only question that you absolutely must answer about any kind of difference of belief.

For example, I've had times in my life where I've eaten

mainly a vegetarian diet, but it's not something that I'm presently doing. At some point, though, my husband stopped eating meat, and because that wasn't where my convictions were at at the moment, I had to ask if this was something he wanted us to do together, because if it was then naturally we would need to talk it through. "Is this something for both of us to get on board with, or is this a 'you' thing?" With his diet, it was totally personal, and that's been no problem for us. I have my 'me' thing, you have your 'you' thing, and with mutual respect it works quite well.

But that's not always the case. When it comes to the matter of faith or religion, for many of us we have strong feelings in one of those directions already. You might consider your faith to be very personal and not really meant to be shared. You may hold your beliefs near and dear to your heart and feel unwilling to share them, let alone compromise on them. On the other hand, it might be imperative to you that you and your partner are on the same page about your religion or faith. Practicing the same faith and sharing it and making it a cornerstone of your life together might be essential to you. That's the same with other beliefs for some people, whether it's political beliefs, dietary choices, or sports team fandom. Maybe you can't imagine being with someone who eats meat or cheers for your rival team, and if you're not interested in compromising then that could definitely be a deal breaker.

So this is the part where we revisit the cultural iceberg, and the thing about beliefs is that they hover around the water line, both visible and invisible. There are parts of them that you can see, whether that's the way someone dresses or their attendance at services in a religious community or a symbol that they like to wear. But there's a lot more that is below the surface that we can't see about beliefs, and that's the stuff that we often aren't even aware of. If it's under the surface, we might not even know that we feel that way. This can be stuff that comes up in your assumptions and your expectations. For example, maybe you don't feel strongly about being a member of faith community and neither you nor your partner practices a faith, but you might have this underlying assumption or expectation that when you have a child, that that child is going to be initiated into your religion.

This can happen, even for people who aren't religious, that they discover some aspect of the tradition is important to them, and is appealing to them as they are becoming parents and raising children. Even with people who are from the same country and culture, you see this, where they aren't actively involved in a religion, but it's important to them that when they have children those children begin attending religious services. It often surprises us to hear people share these plans and feelings with us, but it comes from such a deep place in that iceberg that it's no wonder we haven't been aware of it when maybe even the person who holds that belief didn't know it existed. So when it comes to determining if a belief is a "me" thing or a "we" thing, we've got to keep the communication lines open, because even if one decision has initially been made, it's still possible for it to change with time.

And of course that same thing can be true about any other belief, with those deep hidden parts suddenly surfacing. Let's take vegetarianism as an example. For some people who eat meat, they might have no problem with being a vegetarian, toy with the idea themselves, or even enjoy meatless Mondays. But that same person might have a visceral reaction if their spouse or child announces that they're done eating meat. That person might suddenly be questioning, "But what about Thanksgiving dinner? What are we going to do?" That may be something they didn't know how much they cared about until they felt like they were losing it. We lose our rationality and fear, "Am I losing my Thanksgiving tradition? But it's really important! You have to eat turkey, or else you won't truly be honoring the memory of the seriously terrible treatment of Native Americans." (Sorry not sorry, but if we're talking about Thanksgiving it's important to be real. I love eating good food with people I love as much as the next gal, but this holiday surely has a terrible origin story.) But it does often happen that these significant cultural days have particular foods attached to them, and the thought of not sharing that with someone we love can be harder to swallow than a turkey bone.

I don't think we should make something like an Easter ham a deal breaker, though. I'm sure for all of us we have differences that would be deal breakers for us with our partners, but I think that we should try to keep that list of deal breakers as short as possible. Ideally, you should be able to write it on a postage stamp. It certainly doesn't need to be a laundry list, full of specifications to check off of everything from eye color to hobbies to GPA. That's just my opinion, that often we don't really know what we need in a relationship, so lists like that just end up being full of the predispositions that we already have, when who knows if that's what's best for us as humans on a journey of lifelong development.

Along with deal breakers, we establish ground rules as a family unit when we answer the question, "Is this a 'me' thing or a 'we' thing?" It's foundational to the relationship that we're building. For some, faith is the foundation of their relationship and for others it's devoted love for their favorite basketball team. But in whatever situation we find ourselves, whatever ground rules we have established, it won't work without compromise, and you are naturally both going to have different thoughts, feelings, and cultural influences at play here. Even if you are members of the same faith, there are still aspects of that faith that attached to it from your culture or from your childhood surroundings, and those things are going to come up in conflicts. If you approach those differences as "my way or the highway," it won't be fodder for great understanding and compromise, but it can be a great experience if you approach it from saying, "As I discover more about myself and as you discover more about yourself, we're going to continue to find ways to compromise and meet in the middle."

If you're coming from two different religions and neither of you wants to convert, then holding onto it as a "we" thing won't be fun for either of you, and I don't recommend spending decades of your life trying to convert your spouse. But if it's something that you can find a way to compromise about, then that might make both of you feel more comfortable. Maybe that means two sets of holidays, or if one of you is a vegetarian then maybe that means sharing more meatless meals together. There are many different ways to make a compromise, and there's no right or wrong way to do it. But keeping that dialogue going, and remembering that with any kind of belief-related compromise, it's always important to be able to reopen the topic for discussion. It's not a matter of the conflict being done and dusted, but it's something we may have to revisit during our own personal evolutions.

For a personal example about this, I had an experience in college when I had what I would call a transformational experience. I was a member of a faith community, and it ended up not being a healthy environment and something that I needed to leave. That was a really important decision for me, and it was hard and complicated in more ways than I care to enumerate here. In more recent years, it has come to light that a number of people had the same or similar experiences and also left that same community. As I was going through that, I was talking with friends of mine from that time. One friend and I were both expressing how grateful we were that we were single during that time because it was so much easier not to be deeply embedded in something that wasn't good for us. We didn't have to talk our decisions over with partners, but, from one day to the next, we could totally change our lives. At the same time, I had so much respect for the couples who were able to leave together, because I imagine in that kind of situation, it can be very difficult to speak up to your partner. If you share a common belief and it's a core tenet of your relationship, then you might not feel like you're allowed to express any hesitations or concerns about it. It's important to remember that if you can't be honest with the person you've chosen to live your life with, then who in your life can you be honest with? Perhaps there's a way to do that, to agree to not judge each other, to give each other the benefit of the doubt, and to remember that you value this relationship more than any other institution. This isn't to say it should be so simple to totally transform your shared core values without checking in with each other; of course that requires conversation. But if you're in an environment or in a community and it's not a great place to be, you want to be able to say that, and you don't want to have your partner be the person that you're putting on a nice face for. You don't want to be holding back your true feelings because you're not sure if they're going to feel the same way.

One approach that might be helpful to navigate a situation where one of you is having questions about some shared belief that you have, is to have somebody mediate it for you. Maybe, if you are vegan and one of you starts having doubts about his or her nutrition then the way you move forward is similar. Perhaps if you share your doubts with your partner, then he or she is going to try to convince you back by showing you videos of slaughterhouses, and it's not going to open up a dialogue. It's just going to create defensiveness and make you resolve to do your own thing that much more strongly. The same things can happen if you bring in outside resources or if you bring in a friend to try to make your point seem stronger. The challenge is to find someone who's going to be impartial. If you're fortunate enough to have them, it's a wonderful gift to have friends who can listen to you impartially and still love both you and your partner, even if you are complaining about the other person. It's not always easy for the people who love us to do that because often, if they feel like we are going to get hurt, they can become Momma Bears. (And no, this doesn't apply only to moms.) My mom is a great example. I adore her, and I know she loves me deeply. And because of that, she is the first person to, if I share something with her that I'm unhappy about, tell me that I deserve better or need to get out of that situation. But there absolutely are people that you can find to help you do this. It may mean finding a professional to work with, someone to act like a SCUBA instructor and hold your hand while you dive down to discover your inner depths. And similar to SCUBA diving, if you don't know how to do it, then it's a great idea to get somebody to help you do it because it's totally possible to navigate these sensitive issues, but it might feel a little scary or dangerous doing it all on your own.

I want to close this section with the reminder that it is important to go into a relationship or into the next stage of your relationship being able to love someone without expecting them to change or expecting that they're going to become somebody different. But at the same time, it's important to also remember that they are going to change in some ways, in ways that you're not even going to be able to predict. So be prepared to love them for who they are without wanting them to change and then also be prepared to love them as they become someone different. As you grow and become someone different, you want that same thing from that person. You don't want them to give up on you as you grow and evolve, reminding you of how much cooler or more fun you were before all of this personal growth nonsense. So it's important to extend that same kindness and grace.

7

COMMUNICATION STYLE

It's important to be aware that we all have different communication styles. This might be something that we already know, and it might be totally new information. If we aren't aware of our own communication style, then it's easy to assume that we just communicate. We just do it in the way that everyone should do it, but in reality there is no right or wrong way to communicate. There are many, many different ways to communicate. There are cultural differences and personal differences in communication, for example, in how direct you want to be or in how much you might prefer to avoid being direct. One person might want to say, "Hey, do this for me. Pick up the plates off the table," whereas someone else might feel more natural to say, "If it's not too much trouble, when you get a chance, could you please pick up the plates off the table?" The message is the same. The idea that you're wanting to communicate that those plates need to get off the table is the same, but the way that you express it might have just a couple words or it might be a couple of sentences long. Neither one of these is right or wrong. One might seem more polite to you, but again, that's our cultural value. In a language where it's implied that you're being polite and "please" and "thank you" are more implied than overtly stated, there's nothing wrong with just directly communicating commands.

Before looking at our partners and the people in our lives and wondering why they communicate the way they do or what is wrong with them, it's important to look at ourselves and try and be clear in how we communicate. We can strive to be more aware of our facial expressions, our tones of voice, and the words that we choose to use. When we try to be more mindful about the way that we communicate and we try to be more gentle or more caring or more attentive, then we start to realize how much our words really count and how much meaning they really convey. And honestly, I tend to believe that the more careful we are in our communication, the more that's what we'll get back. We will no longer be lashing out in conversation and starting arguments over tones and reactions but instead, we will be more carefully evaluating the way that we present ourselves in a conversation, in a disagreement, or in a discussion.

Listen to Understand

The first important thing about communicating is to learn to listen to understand rather than listening because you're waiting for your turn to speak. This is something that many, many of us struggle with. How often have you found yourself in a conversation with someone and realized that you didn't really know what they had just said because you were thinking about a rebuttal to something that you didn't agree with that they'd said earlier? This advice to listen is really going to be useful no matter who you are, no matter what your relationship is, but I think it's especially true with a relationship where there are different languages at play.

When there's a language barrier, is the nuanced understanding of language really equal on both sides? It's all the more important to truly listen to understand. So when your partner says something to you, listen deeply and carefully and try your best to understand what message it is that he or she is trying to convey. It can be helpful in this to ask, "Is this what you said? Is this what you meant?" This is the idea of reflective listening, to say, "I think what you're telling me is _____." That way you're communicating to your partner what you think that they're saying and they can confirm or deny.

Don't Take it Personally

We also have the idea of not taking things personally and considering, "What else could it be?" This is something that I read years ago in an article on Tiny Buddha. The idea was when something happens and it triggers you to ask yourself what else could it be? Because your first thought of course is to interpret it immediately and to take it personally. For example, if someone sends you an email and their tone sounds brusque or harsh, well, what clse could it be? Did they mean it that way? Did they intend to upset you or were they writing this email in a hurry because maybe they were on a subway and they were starting to feel a little motion sick and they wanted to communicate the message in the email to you as quickly as possible?

With your partner, maybe he or she says something to you that really hurts you because it reminds you of your childhood. Maybe someone says to you, "We need to talk." Now for how many of us does that phrase "we need to talk," stir up feelings of anxiety and fear and foreboding? Something bad is going to happen. But maybe your partner didn't mean it that way. Maybe they have a story they need to tell you. Maybe something happened at work. Maybe they have to remember to relay a message to you from someone else. It can mean so many things beyond jumping to conclusions and assuming the worst. So the most important thing is to remember not to take things personally, to try to separate the meaning from the emotion and to always, always give the benefit of the doubt.

Self-Assessment

As we learn more and more about ourselves, we find labels to apply to the ways in which we are unique. From Meyers-Briggs types to Enneagram numbers and everything in between, it gets easier and easier to put labels on yourself and figure out who the heck you are.

I know some people consider this to be a type of ego stroking and something with very little point in the real world; I am not one of those people. As much as I enjoy finding out which Hogwarts house I would be in or which city I should retire to, the actual study-based assessments out there go so much further than just giving me a cute line to add to my social media profiles (and I'm a Ravenclaw, in case you were wondering). Personality assessments for individuals, like Meyers-Briggs and the Enneagram help us to understand how we perceive and move through the world, but more importantly than that, they help us become more aware of how we relate to others and where our differences might come from in the first place. Without a level of self awareness, it is hard to address conflict and reach true compromise that works for both people. The same is true for something that helps us better understand how we relate to each other, focusing on the interactions between two people and how both of them give and receive love.

Culture Isn't the Only Source of Difference

Let's dive deeper into the whole personality discovery topic. I have personally found immense value in learning about myself. I like to know that I am an INFJ, who's driven by causes, speaking up for what I believe in, and maybe not great at being around others for any length of time without needing to retreat. It's a fun way to identify myself, but it also serves me to know that there are 15 other combinations of letters in the Meyers-Briggs world, and that the way we perceive and experience the world differently may be a source of conflict between us. For example, my husband and I only have one letter different in our Meyers-Briggs types, but it's a significant one in my eyes. While I'm an introvert who craves alone time and is sensitive to sounds, crowds, and stimuli, he's an extrovert who gets enjoyment out of all the things that I can only consume in small quantities.

By that same token, the Enneagram has been really interesting to me lately. I am a type 5, the observer or the investigator, driven by an almost primal desire to satisfy my curiosity and always seeking information. My husband is a 9, a peacemaker, driven by a desire for inner and outer peace. This is really important for both of us to know. On his spiritual journey, he has been talking a lot about the importance of listening to your heart and not just your head, which is something that I (and the 20 open tabs on my browser) fundamentally struggle with. While I opt for decisive action, he is more inclined to let ideas marinate. Either one of us could easily attack the other one for not being like us, if we perceived our way of being as the only right way. That's the beauty of learning about this personality stuff, though — it gets harder and harder to judge and attack.

That's not to say that our scores on our assessments should define or determine our limitations. We can always go beyond what we learn about ourselves, and hopefully the information that we gain helps us find the best way for us to do that. For example, if I want to learn a new skill that doesn't come to me naturally, I can tap into my innate tendencies to do it in a way that suits me. Maybe skills like sales or marketing don't come along with my built-in personality traits, but guess what? They are both skills that can be learned, and if the motivation is right, then I will be driven to learn them. I find a purpose (to satisfy the INFJ in me) and I quickly research the best course or methodology (to satisfy the 5) and then get to work.

I share all of this because it's easy to forget that we are individuals in a relationship when we come from different cultures. We can get so focused on the differences between our countries and upbringings that we forget that there is great variety within the human experience in addition to and despite culture. Rather than spending your whole life trying to learn about your partner's country's history or pop culture memes (and sure, do that, too), why not do some personal development work together as individuals? Get to know yourself, learn about who you are, what drives you, what you struggle with, and if your partner is willing, have them do the same. Come together and share what you've learned. It's fascinating to find how your differences guide your interactions, and there is limitless information available to help you find your way forward.

Learn How You Give and Receive Love

Along with all of this, it is important to learn how both of you give and receive love. Think about this: when was the last time you really felt like someone loved you? What did that person do for you? Did you receive a love note, or a gift, or did they simply spend time with you doing a shared activity? Research about love languages is everywhere these days, but it's still easy to overlook their application in our lives. Do some journaling, asking yourself about the times you've felt loved and what that looked like. Again, ask your partner to do the same. Come together and share notes. Maybe one of you loves to receive gifts, while the other is all about quality time. Talk through how to take care of both of your needs. Even if you are the best gift giver ever, if your partner would rather spend the day hiking with you, then that's going to be a better use of your time than shutting yourself in your office and hunting through the Internet for just the right birthday present.

Love involves compromise, and that may mean expressing love in a way that doesn't come naturally to you. But hey, if you're in an intercultural relationship, it's likely you're already navigating two or more languages in your relationship. It can't hurt to add love languages in to the mix, too. You may find it easier to learn a new way to express love than to master a new grammar or writing system. In fact, I'd suggest rather than focusing on only one primary love language for each of you to work on incorporating all of them into your life together. Try to change up the ways you express love and the activities that you do together. Routine may be good for your personal growth, but keeping things fresh and interesting is imperative in a long-term relationship.

8

SENSITIVE SUBJECTS

Now that we've covered both religion (the first of the typically taboo topics) and communication style, let's continue communicating with some other topics that are often considered inappropriate to discuss: finances and intimacy.

Finances

Clear communication is imperative to navigating finances as a couple. We want to avoid conflict that comes, as always, from having expectations that aren't communicated clearly, as often tends to be an issue.

There's a lot of mindset work that needs to happen before we can really have clear conversations about what our feelings are on money. There are a ton of great resources out there to help each of us individually work through money mindset issues, so I'm not going to dive into that too much here. What I will say is that the feelings that we have about money do tend to be deeply ingrained from our childhood. That comes from our culture, whether it's the culture of our family, the culture that's presented on movies and TV, or the culture that we're absorbing from the whole world around us. That plays a huge role in how we feel about money. Do we feel secure that we will have enough? Do we feel insecure that we won't have enough? Do we feel like debt is a normal, natural thing to experience at times in your life? Or do we feel like it's something that absolutely must be avoided? What about spending versus saving? If we have extra money, are we going to spend it on something? Or are we going to save it for a rainy day or for a special occasion? What's our plan there?

We can also think about giving. Is that an important part of my culture or yours? Is that something that we're expected to do maybe based on religious or spiritual beliefs? Or is that a completely unfamiliar concept?

Getting into these topics yourself first is going to help you understand where your thoughts and feelings come from. And then that can be the beginning of having a conversation about it.

Conversation about money can be really uncomfortable for many of us. Like intimacy, both topics are difficult for people to talk about, especially when you are closely connected with someone. With money, this may look like your lives being merged, so your views about money can't just be pushed under the rug. Maybe they could be when you were dating and had your own places, but once you start talking about marriage, living together, and having a future together, it's really essential to get into money matters.

Before we get into our own mindset, we can find ourselves having lots of fights about stuff. Maybe your partner spends money on something that you didn't think was reasonable. But instead of understanding that, and realizing that you have a fear of not having enough money, you have this bad feeling in your stomach, like a lack of security, like a worry saying, "Oh no, this is a really bad thing." You worry that it's a pattern that's going to always repeat itself, and so you lash out based on what you're afraid of, something that might happen in the future, instead of making it about what it is right now. What it is right now might just be $50 to spend on a hobby, but in your mind, because you're coming from this deep place of fear of scarcity and not having enough, it feels more like a habit, it's thousands of dollars down the drain, it's your savings emptied out...it's extreme. But until you understand that, it's hard to see how extreme it is.

One thing that can be really helpful, one of the most helpful things for us in our relationship, when we started talking about money was making a budget. That may sound silly to some people. A budget is an interesting thing, because a lot of people swear by it to live, but also a lot of people are kind of oblivious to the concept, or just feel like it's not for them or they just aren't interested.

I'll talk about our understanding of it here a bit. There are definitely a lot of great teachers out there teaching about how to do this well, so I'm not going to give you the breakdown of what I think you should be saving or spending on different things, because it is not my area of expertise. But what I can say is this: it is essential if you're sharing finances with someone to talk about your expectations for what those finances get spent on. Especially if you both have access to the same accounts, you need to be communicating openly and clearly about what money is for what purpose. If you have more money than you could possibly need, even then it's good to talk about this. You might feel like you have more than enough, but when you don't communicate and if, for example, one of you buys an expensive plane ticket or a car or splurges on a vacation, these "little" habits can add up. Some habits are smaller than others, and for some people buying a car is a little habit. But the reality for most folks reading this book, I think, is that they are not in a situation where they're saying, "Oh dang, I just have too much money. Maybe this coach can teach me how to manage it."

So if you don't have a framework laid out for where your money comes from and where it goes, then that's going to be the first most important step. Doing this alleviates a lot of stress and it gets you on the same team about facing a common enemy, your enemy in this case being scarcity, not having enough, debt, or whatever it is for you that you want to avoid. Maybe your common enemy is a fear of not being able to retire or take care of yourselves if one of you gets sick. Maybe you don't like the word "enemy" since it's such a negative term, so maybe you prefer to have a common goal. And maybe your common goal is to retire or it's to be able to quit your jobs and be your own boss or be location independent.

Being on the same page is key, so how do you get there? Well, keeping in mind that your goal is to be on the same page and on the same team, the way to get there is not to sit your partner down and say, "Why did you spend this money on this frivolous thing? Why did you do this, I'm worried about money!" I have made this mistake, not in those exact words, and I like to think I was a little more gentle than that. But in the past, it's been too easy for me to see the fault in my partner and to say, "You bought the fancy almonds instead of the regular ones and gosh, I'm worried about that expensive habit forming there." And it was easy to feel this without realizing that there were things that I was doing and financial decisions I was making that I did not examine with the same scrutiny.

That's just me being honest with you all. I know it's not a good look, but I think it's a relatable thing that many of us do. It's much easier to see the fault in someone else than to see it in ourselves. And the odds are the things that we're noticing about our partners that are annoying or upsetting us may be things that we are also doing, and that might be why they're annoying us or upsetting us.

So instead of coming at this problem on the offensive, I would recommend coming at it from a proactive, defensive kind of approach. I don't mean defensive like when you lash out at someone for questioning a decision you made. I mean defensive more like the two of you are forming the defense so that your enemy won't be able to break that line. So this is where finding a budget or template online can be really helpful. You can say, "Hey, I found this great resource about budgeting. And you know what's crazy is I realize I've never really done that." In this way, you're positioning yourself not as the expert saying, "I know how to do this, I want to do this, and you need to get on board." Instead, you are positioning it as, "Hey, this would be good for us. And I don't really know how to do it myself, but let's figure it out together."

Now, I don't mean this at all, in no way, that if you're a woman reading this book, you should dumb yourself down or that you need to manipulate someone into being on board with what you think you should be doing. Not at all. I just mean that for any suggestion of change in a relationship, the partner who wants that change to be made is going to have a lot more success with getting that change made if he or she approaches it as a humble student interested in learning and growing together, rather than as an enlightened master, saying, "Do this my way or else there's going to be resistance."

The beauty of setting goals as a couple is being able to celebrate every success along the way together. And at the same time, when there are setbacks, you're able to remind each other that it's temporary, it's not the end of the world, you haven't failed, and you'll try again another day. So I highly, highly recommend this in other areas of your life, too. But for this section, let's just focus on finances and getting on the same team. I don't have any other hard and fast rules — I won't tell you that you must avoid debt at all costs or that you must donate X percentage of your income or save Y percentage. Those are rules to take on on your own or according to the teacher that you like listening to. But the non negotiable that you get from me is simply that you've got to, got to, GOT TO be on the same page and fighting towards the same goal. Of course, you may need professional help if there are any kind of addiction issues, gambling, shopping, or otherwise, that are working against you. But to close this section, have that conversation, make that budget, and find your own path towards peaceful financial coexistence in your little family.

Intimacy

One really imperatively important aspect of communication that is so important that I'm even giving it its own sub-chapter is intimacy. Now, yes I do largely mean intimacy in terms of sexuality, but there's a reason I didn't call this chapter just straight up "doing sex" or whatever because I'm not a sex therapist. I'm not into talking about the mechanics with you, but I do think it's really important to touch on the communication aspect of it because this may have extra layers of complication if you add into it multiple languages, different cultural values, and taboos around talking about things that all combine to really not be in your favor.

To start with first of all, many, many, many of us are not comfortable talking about intimacy or sex, and certainly not talking about the things that we like or that we don't like. Many problems in relationships are created by the expectation that things in this area of our lives will just work without us having to talk about them. We see the way sexual intimacy works in pop culture and TV shows, we watch the movies we watch, and we rarely see awkward conversations or discussions about birth control or what happens when things don't go as planned. This is all the more reason why it's important to break down our own barriers around being able to talk about these things. When have issues, especially communication issues, gone away on their own without some hard work, some awkward conversation and caring enough to do both of those things?

First and foremost, you've got to know what it is that you want to express. If you have a desire, it's the same thing as having an expectation. If you keep it to yourself and expect the other person to understand it, that's not fair. That's not playing fair, that's not fighting fair if it ends up causing a conflict, and it's just not a great strategy to take in any kind of conflict or challenge in a relationship. It's the same as if there's a chore that you expect your partner to do around the house, but you don't tell him or her about it and then you're upset when they don't do it. Well, you have to take a majority of the responsibility for not communicating that you expected it to be done.

The same thing is going to be true with intimacy. If there is something that you don't like or something that you do like and you're hoping that your partner is just going to figure it out on his or her own without you expressing it clearly and then you're left feeling disappointed, hurt or unsatisfied because things aren't happening that way, you've got to take at least partial responsibility for that. Honestly, I would say you're going to take the majority of the responsibility because we don't come into this life with a fully equipped toolkit for these kinds of things. We don't get a manual that says, "This is how to talk to your partner about your sexual boundaries or what you're comfortable with or what you like or any of that kind of stuff." Oftentimes we don't even know what it is that we like or need, so how can we even begin to express it if we don't know what it is?

Figuring out for yourself what this is and then clearly communicating it is the challenge. This is a topic that we really like to tread around very lightly and use euphemisms and kind of flowery language to make something sound prettier or sexier than it is, but that's not the way you're going to get your needs or your wants communicated clearly. So many of those euphemisms and those flowery words that we use are rooted in our culture and in our language, and if you don't share culture with someone and if you don't share a common language, then how are they meant to understand what you're saying?

Now this is going to sound like a really awkward thing to suggest, but what I suggest is rather than saying something that you think would be a great line in a romance novel, use words that you might see in a textbook. Be very clear with what you're saying. There are boundary issues in intimacy that if you're not clear, it might sound like you're agreeing to something that you're not agreeing to, so you've got to be crystal crystal clear. Now let go of your hangups about this. Your grandparents or your pastor or the government aren't in your bedroom listening to the things that you're saying. So say the things that you need to say. This is an experience that should be special, should be joyful, should be fun and if you are too afraid to say what you need to say to make it that for you, then what a waste. This is a gift. This is something for us to experience, to enjoy, and if the only thing separating you from a great experience is forming your mouth into the shape of a few awkward words and vibrating your vocal chords to make them come out, well, think about it like that — mechanically. That's the same thing that I just did writing that sentence. I didn't say "shout it from the rooftops," I said "vibrate your vocal chords, move your tongue, shape your lips and make the sound come out that says the right word to convey the meaning that you want to convey." That's all it is.

We attach a lot of significance and a lot of meaning to these things, to this topic in particular, but it's just vocal chords vibrating and words coming out. So practice it. Practice saying what you've got to say. Practice talking about what you need to talk about. Practice doing the thing. And I don't think there's anyone who really knows their stuff about intimacy who would tell you your relationship or your sex life might get worse if you talk about it. I think everyone out there in the field who's preaching on this topic, and especially those who are talking about women and intimacy, everyone would say you've got to speak up for yourself. No one else is going to do it. No one else knows you or your body or your needs like you do, so be your own champion, be your own advocate, and say what you need to say.

9

GEOGRAPHY

Don't Assume

This advice is so important that I probably should have included it in every chapter: "Don't assume." When it comes to making decisions that will affect both you and your partner (and your future family, should you have one), they absolutely cannot be made unilaterally. When you are deciding where you will live together, remember that it is, in fact, a decision. Even if the two of you have only lived together in one country ever, don't assume that that is always the way both of you will feel. Let's say, for example, that your partner is an expat in your country. Even if you've been together there for five years, don't assume that that means he or she will never be interested in returning to his or her country of origin. Maybe he always intended to spend a few years overseas and then return home — or at least always saw himself retiring in his hometown. These are important things to know. Most couples will not choose to have a long-distance relationship, separated by an ocean, and being on the same page about where you will live is really the only way to avoid this.

When my husband and I began our relationship, I was living in Turkey and had been living away from my home country on and off for around seven years. As our relationship got more serious, it felt so natural to me to start to want to return home. Though I'd been happy in my explorations, I missed seeing different developmental stages with my nieces and nephews, and losing a beloved grandparent while 5,000 miles away caused some major priority shifting. Of course there was also the contributing factor that no one in my family had been able to meet my then-boyfriend, other than via Skype.

Consider All Your Options

There are multiple ways to be together as an international couple. This is one of the most exciting things to me, though I know that it can be a source of stress for many of us, too. At first glance, it may feel like your options are limited: my country or my partner's. We weigh those two countries against each other and pick the one that is the best for both of us (likely in terms of our careers, because what else can we be quite that objective about?). We use our vacations to visit the other partner's family, and one of us resigns himself or herself to the idea of living away from "home." There are other creative ways to solve this problem, and I'll share a few of them here.

Pick a third country

In the third episode of the Borderless Stories Podcast, I spoke with an old acquaintance of mine, Tim. Tim and his wife are from Germany and Norway, respectively, and made a conscious decision to live in Denmark. When he explained this decision, he talked about how difficult it can be to not take your partner's complaints personally when they are living in your country. The experience of being expats together can bring you together in unexpected ways as you both navigate the challenges of living in a new culture. Granted, this option is easier for some than others. As Tim explained, in Europe there is freedom of movement, which made it easy for them to move to a country where neither one of them were citizens. If that is not an option, there is the possibility that one of you could look for an employment contract in another country. That would make the other one the trailing spouse, which could pose challenges finding work. Naturally there are pros and cons to this option, but it's worth considering if you find it really difficult to decide between your countries.

Split your time

This is the best option to appease two sets of families (especially if your parents become grandparents and don't want you to keep those kiddos away from them). You may opt to spend the school year in one country and the summer in the other. That's one way to keep education consistent for your children, while still regularly visiting family and exposing them to the other country's language. If you can find a way to make it work for your work/career, you could evenly split your time between the two countries. Maybe you could spend 6 months at your office in one country and the other 6 months working remotely. Of course, this decision would have to be made with an employer, and you may have to get creative with the timing. Be sure that you are in country during the biggest parts of your work year — no missing the board meeting or biggest sale of the year, for example. Additionally, you could also split your time over years — a few years in one country, then a few in the other.

Become location-independent

It seems that more and more work can be done remotely these days. While I'd always dreamed of working from home (homebody since I was just a tiny child), I hear about more and more people in different, diverse industries doing this now. Perhaps you can find a full-time remote position or consider freelancing in your field. If you are able to work for yourself in a way that supports your family, then that may be the most perfect solution of all. Please consider for this option that your taxes may be complicated, so I'm certainly not going to advise you on them. But I would suggest that you talk with a professional to be sure that you are toeing the line and claiming your income in the place(s) where you need to claim it.

When we knew we wanted to make a change but still be together, we considered a whole slew of options for where to go and what to do next. We compared lists of places where both of us could travel and work relatively easily with our different passports. This was a great clue to the privilege that I had with my American passport.

We knew it would be relatively difficult for Hüseyin to come to the US, but we entertained the idea of moving somewhere in Latin America so that at least we would be in a similar time zone as my family and a fairly short trip away. As an added bonus, I'd be able to use my getting-steadily-rustier Spanish.

This option didn't pan out for us for a number of reasons. For one thing, it is disappointingly difficult for a non-native English teacher to find gainful employment teaching English. Overtly blaming this on my husband's "thick accent" seems bizarre to me, especially when the reality is that the majority of people who speak English speak it as a second or additional language. I can't help but wonder if we'll ever get to the point as a society where formal training as an English teacher or performance on a standardized test is weighted more heavily than simply being a native speaker.

The one job offer that "we" got turned out to be a job just for me, while Hüseyin could be a long-term volunteer at the same school. At first glance, this isn't a great deal, but it turned out to be like a really terrible impressionist painting that got even worse on close inspection. Not only would only one of us be earning an income, but then we were told that the best option for us being able to be together for this contract was a spousal visa. Never mind the fact that at the time of this application, we were in a committed relationship with no plans to get married prior to accepting this job. So these are some considerations to keep in mind — it's up to the two of you to do all the research about visas and logistics because it's possible an employer will tell you what you want to hear. I've heard of companies failing to secure employment visas for their international workers, resulting in sketchy situations where work is being done on tourist visas, which is ultimately not sustainable in most cases. It can result in you having to leave a country and in worst cases not being able to return.

10

LANGUAGE

For many people in intercultural relationships, two (or more) languages give way to one dominant language being spoken in the home. If this is the case in your home and family, then you may wonder why you should even bother to learn your partner's language. If he or she speaks your language fluently and your relationship's entire history has happened in that language, then what is even the point of sitting down with vocabulary flashcards and grammar workbooks? In addition, you may believe that you aren't good at languages, so it is only natural that your smart, linguistically gifted partner be the one to take on language responsibilities.

If this is your reality, I'm not judging. The vast majority of my marriage has happened in English, and I am so grateful for the education and intellect that made it possible for my husband to learn our shared language. Meeting past English teachers of his, I want to fawn over them with gratitude — after all, without them, we'd be left conducting our relationship entirely in Turkish. Based on my current abilities at the time of publication, that would mean little more than listing fruits and vegetables and nonsensical profanity.

This isn't to say that because I struggle with Turkish I think we should all have a free pass to speak English all the time. Rather, I share it to say that I know learning a language is hard but I truly believe it is worth doing. The benefits of studying (and maybe even someday mastering) your partner's language are social, relational, personal, and cognitive. How many other academic endeavors can make all those claims?

Social

While your partner may speak your language fluently, it is unlikely that every member of his/her family or friend group is able to do the same. Leaving your partner in the translator role indefinitely can be exhausting for him or her. Undoubtedly, it would be a nice break for your spouse to kick back and relax while you crack jokes with his cousin or take a quick trip to the store with her mom without both of you perpetually glancing at your translator in confusion. This communicates to your extended relative/friend network that you care about them in a way that is impossible to do without cracking open a textbook or an app and actually learning a little.

Relational

In addition to making your partner's loved ones feel like they matter to you, you'll also be demonstrating a level of love and commitment to your partner that he or she is unlikely to overlook. If you don't believe me, put yourself in his or her shoes. If you had been communicating entirely in a second language with the person you love most in this world, occasionally experiencing the frustration of being unable to express yourself in exactly the right words, how would you feel if that person started taking steps to make it possible for you to be able to express yourself in the language you've grown up with? I imagine that feels like relief and appreciation. While you know it won't be an immediate solution, taking that first step is a beautiful thing.

Personal

Do you feel like you can fully be yourself when you are unable to communicate? I don't know if this is the same for everyone else, but when I am in an environment where everyone is speaking Turkish, I end up feeling like I haven't been able to show up to that situation as fully myself. First, I avoid engaging as much as I normally would, usually because I don't want people to notice that I'm struggling to communicate, and the best way to do that is to look like I am engaged in something else, off in my own little world but not bored. I end up focusing so much on what my face must look like that I miss out on making any real connections. In a language where I am comfortable, I love making people laugh, but in an uncomfortable language setting, I withdraw and remind myself more of the shy little girl that I used to be than the confident woman I have become with the passage of a few decades. Because of this, I believe that as my language abilities grow, I'd feel an increased sense of being true to myself as well as the freedom of not being so dependent and reliant on my husband.

Cognitive

The research is in, and the reality of studying an additional language and someday becoming bilingual is that it is damn good for your brain. Think about the people in your life who start doing sudoku puzzles or taking piano lessons with the hope of keeping their brains "fresh." Studying a language is great for a brain, and the cognitive benefits are astounding and surprising.

How the Heck to Learn a Language

To start with, think about your learning style. How have you enjoyed learning things in the past? Are you a visual or auditory learner? Do you prefer to listen to podcasts or read books? Do you prefer theory or practice? Do you want to listen to someone explain rules to you, or do you want to hop in a lab and try to figure it out by trial and error?

These questions will help you figure out your next steps. If you are an auditory learner, it would be a great idea to start with some simple podcasts, classical apps (I remember language-learning cassettes from my youth, so there must be an equivalent in the post-cassette era), and songs in your target language. Get your ears tuned to listening and listening carefully (no more just "tuning it out.") If, in contrast, you prefer learning visually, start with a workbook or some authentic materials (kids' books would be a great start!) in your partners' language. And no, I haven't forgotten kinesthetic learners, either.

If you can find ways to get active while engaging with the language, that'd be a great place to start. If you live in a place where there is a community of people speaking your target language, maybe you can find some new friends to play sports with or you can get involved with a running group, community band, or basically any place looking for volunteers.

Before I go on, I want to emphasize that while we all have preferences for how we learn, there are benefits for everyone of taking in content in your target language in various forms. Yes, you may prefer to read books rather than listen to podcasts or get active in a community. But all of these things offer additional exposure to the language that you want to learn, and in turn they will develop your skills far more together than any one of them could independently.

Finally, it's essential to actually use the language that you are studying — after all, there is a difference between theory and practice. If you are able to flip through a stack of flashcards really quickly without making a sound, that's great. But are you sure that you really know how to pronounce all of those words? Even more importantly, if you heard them in authentic conversation, would you recognize them? That's why we've got to take what we're learning from the controlled environment of our own textbooks, apps, and quiet desks to the messy, awkward situations where we'll actually be using (and cementing) what we're learning.

11

IMMIGRATION

To Hire a Lawyer or Not to Hire a Lawyer

Many intercultural couples may also be international couples and may therefore face the challenges of navigating immigration together. If you've been fortunate enough to meet your partner while you both already had legal status in the same country, then this section may not apply to you. For those who have yet to figure out a way to be together long term in the same country, you'll absolutely want to read this.

When you are trying to figure out how to join your partner in his or her country or bring him or her to your country, the legality of it can be daunting. If, for example, you are in the United States and are trying to find a way to be together, you may initially consider other ways for your partner to immigrate, especially if you aren't yet ready to get married. Securing an employment visa may be incredibly difficult, and by the same token a student visa may end with your partner being in a prohibitively expensive program. While my husband and I initially considered both of these options, the conclusion of our discussion ended up being that we would need to have our decision to be in the same country be based solely on our relationship. With that, our options were to get a fiance visa or a spousal visa. As he had not yet met my family in person, it felt uncomfortable to me to come back home married, and additionally the fiance visa applications were being processed a bit more quickly than spousal visas, at least at that time. Thus, we began the process.

One thing that is true of the fiance visa process that I'm certain is true of a spousal visa process as well is that, from start to finish, there is nothing simple about it. In the United States, the application itself is many pages long, with a separate document of instructions that is approximately the same length. Even at first glance, it is daunting to imagine mere mortals like us completing the process, and it's hard to believe that anyone does it without hiring a lawyer.

I don't advise either hiring a lawyer or not hiring a lawyer as a uniform solution for everyone in the fiance or spousal visa process. In fact, I don't offer any legal advice at all because I am certainly not qualified to do that. Instead, I will tell you our story and the factors that played into our decision. The only thing I will say with certainty is that there is no absolute, universal right decision for everyone as to whether to hire a lawyer or not.

For my husband and I, after doing some initial research, I decided that I could complete the paperwork for our process myself without hiring a lawyer to do it for me. As far as I could tell, hiring a lawyer wouldn't impact the length of the process, and as Turkey was not considered a "high fraud" country by USCIS, I wasn't overly concerned about our chances of being accepted or rejected. Granted, at many points throughout the process, people in my life either assumed I had hired a lawyer or advised me that I must hire one. I came away with the conclusion that horror stories about immigration are not that different from horror stories about wisdom tooth removal or childbirth: everyone has a story to share, and somehow telling them that you are about to go through that experience yourself makes them feel the need to share it with you. Just as someone about to have four teeth extracted doesn't want to hear about the time you got dry socket, someone waiting to hear back from USCIS doesn't want to hear about what went wrong with your cousin's friend's roommate's fiance visa. If there is nothing to do but wait, then by all means do not offer any advice or input.

There are some topics that may be especially worth considering when you are making the decision about hiring a lawyer or not.

To start with, consider your personal history and circumstances. Where are you or your partner from? If you are from a country that is considered "high fraud" by USCIS, then there may be more difficulty in securing that visa. The requirements for the interview portion of the fiance visa process (and I would assume the spousal visa process as well) vary from country to country, so they may be more lax or stringent depending on where you are from. If you believe that your case may be taken more seriously in a "high fraud" country with the assistance of a lawyer, then by all means, explore that option. A lawyer cannot guarantee acceptance of your application (so certainly be wary if they do guarantee that), but their presence may provide a helpful perspective and peace of mind.

Additionally, what about you and your partner as individuals? Is this the first marriage for both of you? How much time have you spent together in person? These questions apply specifically to the fiance visa process. Due to the nature of the visa, which allows a non-citizen to enter the US and marry his or her fiance within 90 days, previous marriages may matter a great deal. If the US citizen in this case has been married before and if those marriages were fiance visa marriages, then they may be examined with a fine tooth comb by USCIS. As well, if the non-citizen partner has been granted visas to the US before, those can help or hinder the application as well. If he or she has previously overstayed a visa, that can have a negative effect on the processing of this visa. In these instances, it may be worth consulting with a lawyer.

Finally, how comfortable are you with the language on the application and instructions? Yes, I know it is in English and that may be your first language — but how comfortable are you with the jargon and technical language being used? Do you glaze over when you read it and find that you haven't absorbed it? Does it make you sweat? If that's the case, there's no shame in hiring someone to help you with it. Whether that be a lawyer or a visa processing service, if the language makes you uncomfortable, then it is an absolutely worthwhile investment to hire someone to help you with it.

In all of these cases and questions, it is ultimately up

to you whether you decide to hire help or not. Be wary of any promises of speed or success, as those things are out of all of our hands and ultimately only up to USCIS. Make the decision that is best for you and your partner, and consider your budget, too. Immigration is not a cheap feat, and it is important to be aware of all of the expenses. You can check USCIS (or the respective department in your own country) for the most up-to-date application fees.

Helpful Resources

Some of the most helpful resources when navigating immigration are other people. Now, I definitely don't mean this in the, "Ask anyone and everyone their opinion and crowdsource your next steps" way. I've previously compared immigration to childbirth and wisdom tooth extraction and you'll surely find the fact that people are ready and willing to share their horror stories with you to be true. This is a bizarre trait we as humans share. When we learn that someone is pregnant, we feel an irresistible compulsion to tell them about the time our friend's sister spent 48 hours in labor. I don't know why we do this, but I do know from my own experience that we also like to do it with immigration. I received unsolicited opinions left and right all throughout the fiance visa process, which are easy enough to take with a grain of salt, but stories about how relationships failed or paperwork got lost definitely didn't inspire confidence.

In my opinion, there are a few places where you can find communities of people who really, truly know what they're talking about and have useful information to share. Those are the various visa forums where others who have gone through the process share their experience, their story, their timeline, and advice for others in the same position. Because visa paperwork and its respective process is unique for each type of visa (and can also vary solely depending on the country of application), it's important to get your information right from the source. Even if someone is applying for the same visa, if they are applying from a different country, the details may be different and may not apply to you. This is all the more true if it's an application for a different visa entirely. Very few facts are universal in the visa process, and that's why it's so important to get information that applies directly to you and your situation.

The forum that I used religiously during our visa journey was called just that: VisaJourney. There are others that exist, I'm sure, but it's my favorite because it's the one I've spent the most time using. I found it by searching various terms related to the K-1 visa process and questions that I had, and since it consistently came up at the top of the search, I spent more and more time perusing its many forums. Being able to find people who were in the same situation (from Turkey, completing the interview in Ankara, etc.) was quite confidence-inspiring. I was able to ask questions and source answers from people who know what they're talking about because they've lived it. That certainly helped me feel more prepared and better equipped for what was coming down the road.

Don't underestimate the information put out by governments, embassies, and consulates, of course. This is typically where the most up-to-date forms and instructions can be found, and forum entries from five years ago may be completely out of date. Check directly with the government website first, and then corroborate and expand on that information by going to the forums for firsthand accounts.

Honesty is Essential

It's important to consider anything that might make your immigration process more complicated than most. This is certainly going to mean having open conversation with your partner about your respective pasts. For example, if you are applying for the K-1 fiance visa, it's essential that both partners know each other's relationship history as pertains to previous marriages. If one of you, perhaps, married at a young age and it didn't last and now you feel embarrassed about it and never told your partner, that won't fly with USCIS. The nature of the application and interview process is to uncover your relationship legitimacy and secret marriages will do the opposite of impressing your interviewer. Not only does this impact your chances of being granted a visa, but much more significantly it can be a major red flag in a relationship. I firmly believe there is never a good time to keep secrets from your partner, but this is even more true during the immigration process than during any other single day or year of your life together. Keeping a secret would be the same as jeopardizing or gambling with your relationship, and it communicates a lack of taking the process seriously and a lack of respect for each other. This is the time to put cultural differences in communication aside and prioritize direct, clear communication over sensitivity or tiptoeing around feelings.

The main thing here will be open, honest communication about your past, as well as your future.

You'll need to talk about past relationships, past visas that were granted, and your plans for the future together. Honestly, entering into a long bureaucratic process to do life together is not something that can (or should) be entered into lightly, so it's really important to take it seriously and leave no stone unturned when it comes to your conversation.

Closing the Distance

When you're planning for your partner to come join you at the end of the immigration process — or at the beginning of it, depending how it looks in your situation, it can be tempting to over prepare. We're so excited to be reunited, and knowing that he or she won't be able to work or might feel out of place in a new country, we try to prepare for every possible situation we might find ourselves in. We seek out communities and activities, we shop for familiar or exciting gifts, and we channel our excitement into planning. But there's only so much that you can do with all of that because ultimately it's up to our partners if they want to partake in the things that we've prepared. They may want to try something totally different, or the transition to life in your country may be so challenging that they just want to withdraw and regroup a bit before emerging into the "real" world. The fact is, there's only so much we can do to prepare and there's a limit to how much it will actually help. So, the challenge is to do only what you can and then to somehow find a way to rest and enjoy and be in the present moment.

We might feel that we'd love to be in that future moment where we are reunited, and that feeling makes us want to organize and prepare, but we have to remember that some of that preparation needs to wait because we need to accept that we can't actually control the situation just by planning every piece of it. Let's make an analogy to illustrate this. Imagine your life with your partner in your country is a salad. Of course you want it to be the best possible salad; you love this person dearly, so of course you want to treat him or her to something special. So, you go get all of the best ingredients, working your way to different grocery stores to pick just exactly what you know will be a really special treat for him or her. You search out things that are really healthy, too, even if you know he or she doesn't necessarily like to eat them — you know what's going to be good for him or her, right? Then you put them all together into this glorious salad...and it sits and sits and sits...and rots before your partner actually arrives to enjoy it. So to you, dear readers, I say, as much as you want to make that salad right now, why don't you instead just make a list of what you want to put in it? You can keep that list someplace safe and go shopping for the ingredients when the time is right and your partner has just arrived or is just about to arrive.

By including your partner in the decisions about how he will spend his time, it's a way for your partner to feel like he or she has autonomy. When we're talking about the K-1 visa immigration process, there is a period of time where he or she might feel stranded because of being unable to work. So your partner is in a situation where there's so much that he or she can't do and so much of that is what gives us a feeling of worth in our cultures. Working and earning an income or traveling freely or driving a car — all of these are things that, without them, can make you feel like you're a prisoner in your own home. It can be especially uncomfortable for people to be stranded at home while their partner is the one earning money, and this can certainly be true along gender lines as well. So, the things that our partners can make decisions about, such as the way they spend their time while we're at the office, for example, are really important. And it's okay if this adjustment happens slower than we want it to, as long as it's driven by our partners.

We can see our planning as a way to show love to our partners, but that can lead to a lot of conflict if we aren't clear with ourselves and with our partners about why we're doing all this planning. Our partners might wonder where we are or what's keeping us so busy, but then the thing that is keeping us away from them or from talking to them is trying to plan their lives in our countries down to the last detail. Research can feel very productive, but it's not always the best use of our time. If it makes the other person feel loved to have us do this for them, well, then that's great. But often it makes us feel like we are doing something loving but it makes the other person feel like we're just ignoring them and wasting time on the Internet.

Let's let our homes be havens for comfort in all the change and transition of immigrating. When everything feels unfamiliar, we can find or create a place that feels peaceful and safe. But this can be another area for us to overly plan and prepare. So, let's not underestimate the power of just being present with our partners. The presence of a familiar, loving person can be incredibly comforting when you're in a completely new situation. When you're there with somebody that you love, it's easier to remember why you are there and to know that you can handle it. So, in your preparations, reign yourself in and remember what's important. You don't need to opt out of all preparations, but you can avoid treating it like you're preparing to rent out a room in your home and you're trying to snag the best possible rating from every stranger who stays there. In that situation, sure, you can anticipate all of their needs and throw in some little extra surprises, too. That's great hospitality, though taken a bit to the extreme. Imagine leaving a booklet for that guest full of ideas that they can fill every minute of their trip with — if that is overkill for them, then it certainly is for the person that you're choosing as your partner in life, too.

12

DISCRIMINATION

For many of us, entering into a relationship with someone from a different racial, religious, or cultural background can expose us to the prejudice that exists in our countries or communities in a way of which we may previously have been blissfully ignorant. As I'm writing this, I hope the relative privilege I enjoy as a white woman in a heteronormative relationship doesn't make this content seem unrelatable to couples coming from a place with less relative privilege. The truth is, I've been on a journey, educating myself about the places where I both benefit from and lack privilege, and my hope for this work is to both raise levels of awareness among those who may not have thought about some of these issues as well as also to offer support to those who may need it. As we explore this topic together, let's start in the same place where all of our personal growth happens: with ourselves.

It is often easier to recognize the places where we don't have privilege than the ones where we do. I think this is human nature — it is easier to accept the ways in which we may identify as being at a disadvantage than to acknowledge the ones where we benefit. When things go well for us, we want to believe that it is only by our own merit that we have succeeded, but when we are struggling, we can acknowledge that the system may actually be against us. I don't say this to attack anyone, but simply to illustrate my own perspective a few short years ago. I didn't deny the challenges of women in the workforce (or even in feeling safe walking through the world in their bodies), as those were things I had directly experienced. I saw the double standards my male and female coworkers experienced and the different opportunities made available to them. I also experienced the heart-racing terror of being followed down a poorly lit road by a man I didn't know. These are fairly commonplace experiences for women, and far worse things happen around the globe on a daily basis.

As much as I accepted the existence of this privilege that I didn't have, at the same time I rarely thought about the ways that I might be in a privileged position in the world. I didn't consider myself wealthy by any stretch of the imagination — I couldn't move out of my parents' house, so how could that be true? I owned my intelligence and charm, and cited any success of mine as directly related to those two things. Sure, I'd been offered nearly every job interview I'd ever had — that was because I was good at interviewing. I'd done well in school from beginning to end — that wasn't always because of how hard I studied, but I considered my intelligence and test-taking abilities as virtues I deserved rather than random traits that had been assigned to me before birth.

The idea of having privilege is uncomfortable, and we show resistance to it when it is first presented. Some of the ways that I've experienced that discomfort (which quickly led to some of the personal growth I treasure the most) have been travel, books, and the people I choose to surround myself with. If you have the means to travel to a country outside of your comfort zone, skip your next luxury vacation and go there instead. If you have preconceived notions about a country and think it's too dangerous, full of ignorance and danger, and basically not worth a visit, I encourage you to do your research and see if it's possible to be surprised and proven wrong. Even if you aren't able to travel to that place, you can read books from local authors or connect with locals on social media. If you're able to travel there, do, but if you aren't financially able or it's too much of a leap out of your comfort zone — then that's where the internet is your friend. Can you find literary fiction written by a local author and set in that country? If non-fiction is more your style, then go for it. I'm a firm believer that a well-written novel can teach you more than a textbook about the culture of the place: nothing beats getting inside the head of the protagonist and experiencing a place through those eyes.

I believe travel and books are such essential pieces of this education about privilege because they open your eyes in so many ways. They make you aware of the commonalities that we all share, which makes it harder to dismiss some countries, cultures, religions, or groups of people as the "other." In turn, this forces us to accept the "othering" we've been doing. If we've been fully aware of it, then it's time to own our prejudice and start doing the work to dismantle it. But if we haven't been aware of it, then cluing ourselves in to our unconscious biases is a great place to start. Before you say, "Oh, I don't see color/sexuality/ability," as an excuse for why this doesn't apply to you, don't. Instead, listen to people from different racial groups, religions, sexualities, gender identities, abilities, and so on. If all your friends look, pray, vote, and move through the world in the same way as you, then it's unlikely that you do see color/sexuality/ability. It doesn't confront you on a daily basis, so on the odd occasion that you run into someone who doesn't fit your same description, they are easy enough to ignore. But if there are people in your life (either in real life or, at the very least, on social media) who occupy spaces you don't, this is a great opportunity to listen and learn. You may very well find that the things that are easy for you to overlook are the same things your friends must pay attention to. They may feel unsafe because of their perceived differences, and it may even be hurtful to them when you dismiss those things as being unimportant. Isn't it, after all, the definition of privilege to be able to choose whether something matters or not, rather than being confronted by it day in and day out?

Confronting Insensitivity

If your partner "passes" as a member of your community, either through language fluency or outward appearance, it may be some time before you experience too much pushback from those around you. The reality is that you are much more likely to hear insensitivity directed your way if you are a mixed race couple or if one or both of you doesn't speak English fluently.

My husband has an accent. (Newsflash: we all do. His just sounds more unusual to a North American ear, but that doesn't make it wrong.) When people don't understand him, I feel myself inwardly cringing, hoping that they won't say something offensive about not being able to understand him. Occasionally, I feel their eyes on mine, as if looking for a translation. I've been asked (in front of him, no less) if I taught him English, which didn't feel great either. Considering that we were together in Turkey for three years prior to our move to the States, I found it strange that people would have more faith in my ability as an English teacher than in his Turkish education for all those years before we met.

That's minor in comparison to what couples from different races experience. I've heard women from various Asian countries commenting on being fetishized, called "exotic," and far worse. There are comments about "mixed babies being the cutest," problematic on so many levels. No one gets to have an opinion on whether you reproduce or not — this is not a decision made by committee. In addition, commenting on someone's race like it's an accessory is bizarre at best and offensive and dangerous at worst.

When confronted with ignorance, it can be easy to want to fight. I get that. And I certainly don't want to add my voice to the mix of well-meaning writers encouraging women to be gentle, kind, and loving to a fault. It can be easy to feel like what has worked for me as a white woman with a relatively easy journey to get where I am is going to universally work for everyone. The truth is that I don't know anything about the experiences of members of groups where I don't belong. So the advice I offer here is intended only for partners of relatively high privilege. For partners who experience discrimination on a daily basis, I only say that I trust your own judgment about the boundaries that you need to have with others in your life. For the partners with more privilege, I'd like to talk about how to be a source of support.

If you find yourself encountering people who look down on your partner for his or her religion, skin color, gender identity, ability, or anything else, it can be easy to want to write that person off. I don't blame you if you do. But if you are able, it may be an effective way to act as an ally to your partner's community if you can invite that person into the conversation, sharing resources with them or drawing their attention to their problematic behavior. I'm not suggesting doing this if someone is violent or threatening. Obviously the safety of your family is more important than any education. But if someone makes a tasteless joke or commits a microaggression, you are in the perfect place to invite them to evolve. You may feel triggered by what they say or do, but ask yourself honestly: would I have laughed at that joke 20 years ago? Have I ever said something like that in my life? I'm not saying this will be universally true for all of us, but many of us have had our eyes opened simply by meeting our partners, so how dare we pretend we were born knowing all of the things that we know? When we refuse to act as allies and instead opt to cut people out of our lives, we are no longer standing between those people and the community we claim to value. If you step out of the way, it is entirely possible that person's jokes or comments will come directly to a community member, who will be fully justified in his or her decision to cut that person out of his or her life. But any work that you can do to raise consciousness levels will ultimately help more than your self righteousness.

Unconscious Bias and Antiracism

Along with becoming aware of privilege and seeking to be a good ally, it's important to do the inner work that helps us become aware of our own biases. The first step is simply admitting that they exist — when we deny that a problem exists it doesn't make it go away. Statements like, "I don't see color" simply give away the fact that your race has never been the cause of a problematic encounter. It doesn't negate the real lived experiences of people of color.

In cases like this, the time spent sharing your opinions would be better spent listening to people of color or people who are part of the community that you are feeling opinionated about. And honestly, it's not even a matter of asking questions — I know for a fact that there are members of every possible community sharing their story right this moment on the internet, ready for you to listen. Find educators who don't look like you or move through the world in the same way that you do, and listen to their story. Become aware of the beliefs and biases you've held in the past and may still have now, and tune in to how these express themselves in your behavior. This is what's going to make it easier for you to invite others into the evolution as you continue to move forward. Rather than looking at folks who make insensitive comments with judgment and disdain, you'll be able to connect with them as a version of who you used to be, perhaps very recently. No one is a lost cause, and you weren't born

"woke." Invite someone to take the first step —
transformational growth can happen more quickly than
you'd expect, and it's a beautiful journey to invite
someone to begin. Let yourself be someone who is ready
to educate and include, rather than someone who
dismisses and "others" a person after seeing them dismiss
and "other." Meet ignorance with an invitation, if you're
in a position of privilege to do so.

It is not enough to merely not be a racist or bigot.
I think to effectively ally with those people groups in
which you aren't a member, we have to actively engage
in the antiracist work. I don't consider myself qualified
to teach this, and honestly there are already likely more
than enough white women speaking out about topics that
we can't understand experientially. Seek out antiracist
educators that resonate with you, and pay those teachers
for their lessons. This is not something to expect our
friends who are minorities to teach us for free, and we
need to invest in this education like it matters to us.

13

FAMILY

Individual and Communal Culture

One major source of conflict for many intercultural couples is the role of family. I've heard people complain that their partner put his or her family's needs over their own, and I've also heard complaints about a partner being too independent and not connected enough with his or her family (or his or her in-laws). It is difficult to navigate this conflict without an understanding of the basic differences between individual and communal cultures.

To start with, let's remember again that no culture or value system is better than any other. All of them have their positives and negatives, and "different" does not equal "negative" or "inferior." The basic family structures that I have firsthand experience with are the individualistic culture of the US and the more traditional family-oriented culture in countries like South Korea and

Turkey. I can't speak about caste systems or cultures that I have not experienced, but I believe even this distinction between individual- and family-orientation is significant enough to be addressed in depth.

In a country like the US with so many different cultures represented, there is no universal experience. I consider my upbringing fairly standard, but I also realize that there are those who experience a family-oriented culture within the US as well. That said, this is my experience: I grew up in a family and community where individualism was a value. I was encouraged to explore my own hobbies and to achieve success in school for my own sake. No one told me I needed to do well to honor my family or so that I could provide for anyone but myself. My parents were proud of me, but they didn't put pressure on me to do or become anything other than I was. Being able to entertain ourselves as kids was a value in our family, too. There's something my dad told me when I was a kid that I started to hear myself say during my years as a teacher, while I apparently slowly turn into my father: "If you're bored, you're boring. It's not my job to entertain you." I think this is what helped me start to develop my own inner world, and my ability to entertain myself for hours on end on a road trip, staring out the window lost in thought. This connects with privacy as well. I was allowed and encouraged to take time alone if I needed it, though prone to depression as I was at a young age, my mom would often come sit with me and see if I needed to talk. This still gave me the autonomy to decide for myself if and when I wanted to share what was going on with me. My privacy wasn't ever invaded, and it was always me who was choosing to spend time with my loved ones, not any pressure or obligation to do so.

As I shift now to talking about family-oriented culture, I hope that my words don't sound judgmental. Even in the previous paragraph, using words like "invade" to talk about privacy sure sounds harsh. It is important to be aware of my own bias, which may have once been unconscious bias and which now I strive to become increasingly aware of. That said, let's move on to family-oriented culture.

In a family-oriented culture, the priority is placed on family units rather than individuals. The relationships which hold us all together are more important than any one person. Multiple generations may live in one house, unlike in an individualistic society where elders may end up living in retirement homes and assisted living facilities. Children may be encouraged to succeed so that they can provide for their families as the generations shift. When immersed in a culture like this, someone from an individualistic background may feel like they aren't getting enough alone time. I find myself wondering at times how introverts function in societies that value togetherness so much.

Marrying into a Family

When you marry someone, the cliche is true that you marry their family, too. Even if your partner is estranged from their family, this is still true. By linking your lives, you are linked to their family, whether that is a lack of close family or the possibility that they will be reunited in the future.

That said, as much as we talk about boundaries, your relationship may be an island, but let's imagine that island is off the coast of a much bigger piece of land, and you'll need to visit that land sometimes, too. Do it on your terms, sure, and don't be pressured to be someone that you aren't or who is outside of your boundaries, but isolating your relationship from the rest of the world isn't a recipe for success.

Get to know your in-laws, and encourage your family to get to know your partner. While these relationships often are based solely on what you have in common (i.e., the person you are married to...), there may be common ground that you can find. Take an interest in each other. What kinds of books are they reading? What movies do they enjoy watching? What kind of work do they do? Where did they grow up, and what stories do they like to tell about their childhood? During the time that my husband and I stayed with my parents (the first two months of our marriage), we watched a lot of movies together, and I think that formed a connection between my husband and my dad. Discovering that they enjoyed the same kinds of stories and could enjoy them without having to have long, in-depth conversations that looked like therapy sessions was good for both of them.

Navigating Conflict

Oh, hey, don't be surprised that conflict is a part of, well, every relationship ever. While you and your partner will no doubt have conflict with each other, on top of that you may have conflict with one or both of your families, too. There are ways to navigate this gracefully, and I hope you'll take note.

First things first, if the conflict happens between your partner and his or her family, tread lightly. Remember that you are related to his or her family by marriage and you don't have the same shared history that your partner does. Barring extreme cases or abuse, don't demonize your partner's family even if that is what he or she is doing. If conflict arises and you've always kind of not liked your in-laws, now is not the time to share that. Don't be a wedge to drive this family further apart, but instead work to be a bridge between the two parts. The odds are that your partner is not going to sever all ties with their family, and when they make peace again, the things that you say or do may bring up some resentment. Listen, and if you need to say something, then reflectively listen. Say to your partner, "It sounds like you felt _____ when _____ happened." This will help him or her to feel listened to and cared for, but it won't result in you trash talking his or her family. When you want to say, "I know, he's the worst!" stop yourself, and ask, "Why do you feel that way?" or, "Why do you think that happened?"

Confused as to why you can't trash talk your in-laws? Let's do a little thought experiment here. Imagine that you're frustrated with your mom and expressing this to your partner. If he says, "I know, she's such a jerk. We don't need to see her anymore," how would you feel? Would you lash out at him and tell him he's overreacting or that he doesn't understand her? My brother and I had a typical sibling relationship growing up — he is a couple years older than me, so we enjoyed hanging out sometimes, but I was often his annoying little sister and got picked on a bit. But the second I came home and told him that another kid at school was picking on me, he was protective to a fault. "I can pick on her; you can't." A great way to find out how loyal your partner is to his or her family is to insult them. And NO, I don't recommend this.

While it may make your partner realize that his parents aren't so bad after all, one of you may be sleeping on the couch for awhile. Remember to listen and ask questions when you want to judge, and hopefully peace will be easier to come by.

I guess the point here is that, as much as it's true that you marry into the whole family, there is also always the in-law dynamic at play. It's no wonder that so many cliches exist about mothers-in-law, or that so many of us have that one problematic person in our lives who's usually related to us by marriage. The saying that you don't get to pick your family applies to the people you're related to by marriage, too. You may choose your spouse, but if you wait until you find the perfect person and the perfect family attached to them, then you'll be waiting a long time. (And also be spending way too long judging others when you could be doing some inner work on yourself.) You can't choose who your siblings marry, who your children marry (unless that's a part of your culture), or who your friends marry, and it's entirely possible that your partner's family is having these same thoughts about you. Rather than focusing on what is wrong with them, be a bigger person and work on what you can control and change about the situation. Time after time, you will find that the only person whose behavior you have any access to the motherboard of is you. Be the best you you can be (and yes, that does include not trash talking your partner's family, even if you swear, "He started it!").

Want Kids?

If you haven't done so already, you and your partner really need to talk about both of your feelings and plans around having children or not. Assuming that you are on the same page or that you'll figure it out later is a recipe for disaster. If you absolutely, positively want to have children, then you need to talk about that before you get married. The same is true if you absolutely, positively don't want to have children. Neither of these are interesting facts about yourself that you should keep secret until you run out of conversation starters. That only works if you both happen to be on the same page, but why risk the implosion of your relationship that could happen if you aren't? When things start to get serious, if you haven't already then you need to have an honest conversation about whether or not you want to have children.

One of you may feel pressure from family or culture to have children and may be obligated to carry on a family name or provide a grandchild for your parents. One of you may feel you don't have parental instincts or not want to be tied down by having a family of your own. Neither of these options are right or wrong, but they are both options. There's nothing wrong with owning your opinion and saying it out loud to your partner — in fact, it's the best way to move the conversation forward.

One important consideration about having children in an intercultural family is the reality of moving (or at least traveling) internationally regularly. You may live in one of your home countries, but you will doubtlessly be visiting the other one, especially if you have family there who would want to spend time with your child. The reality of this international air travel is that it is expensive and uncomfortable, so it is important to think about where you would want to give birth to your child and how easy it would be for family members to come visit you as opposed to you traveling to see them.

If you choose to have a large family, the expense of international travel may be restrictive. You may be limited to visiting your family or in-laws every other year or only part of your family traveling at a time. This makes the decision of where to live a bit more complicated — if you choose one of your countries, then your family who lives there will appreciate having you close, but the other side of your family may feel slighted or struggle to connect with you. Of course, no one else's desires are as important as your nuclear family being on the same page, but if you are able to and interested in considering how others are going to perceive your decision, this is worth thinking about.

In addition, if you're thinking that a solution is to split your time between the two countries, then you will also need to consider how this will affect your child's education. Will they spend a full school year in one school, or will they be leaving before it is finished? If they spend a few years in one country and then move to the other, are their language and social skills likely to be sufficient to do this with ease? Are you okay with the curriculum taught in the public schools in both countries, or would you need to explore private schools or homeschooling? Is homeschooling even an option for you? Some of these questions may seem like they are way down the road, but I like to be nothing if not well prepared.

Pets

Now, pets don't specifically relate only to children, but

this seemed like as good a place as any to stick these thoughts in. Many families enjoy having family pets, and growing up with a dog or a cat can make for a lot of sweet memories. But think about the realities of traveling with a pet (or leaving it behind). While it is true that you might be able to travel with your pet after certifying it as an emotional support animal, how does international travel work? Would it need to be quarantined or have any special veterinary checks done? How long is the flight, and would that be hard on your pet? If you're not able to fly with it, how long are you likely to go for, and would you be able to find someone to care for it for that time? If you don't think about these things, you may end up having to give up that pet, so I implore you to think hard on this. I am not a proponent of abandoning family members (duh), and if I never see another picture of a puppy with sad eyes who got left behind by his owners, then it'll still be too soon. Please remember that pets are not accessories or temporary sources of entertainment. They require love and commitment and when they trust us to give it to them then we should do our absolute best to do just that.

Language

Finally, consider how you would raise children in terms of language. If there is one primary language of your relationship, would you raise them to know only that language? If so, are there family members who would not be able to communicate with them? If that's the case, it is likely to be a source of conflict. To avoid that, is raising them bilingually an option? One of the most common tactics for raising bilingual children is when one parent speaks one language and the other parent speaks the other. This could be challenging if you don't both speak both languages, but luckily you just read the chapter on language, so you should at least be beginning to remedy that situation.

It is a great demonstration of respect to both sides of your family to value their languages equally. There is no harm in growing up bilingually, and in fact it is shown to have a number of benefits. Not only will your child be able to communicate with more people (including family), but he or she will have cognitive benefits which include but are not limited to a lower risk of dementia later in life. Some may worry that the child will be confused, but the reality is that language acquisition and active language learning are two different things. Your child won't be translating words as a youngster; he'll be picking up words and sounds all around him and slowly (or quickly) finding their place in his framework. He or she may start speaking a little later than you'd expect but that is not necessarily cause for alarm. There is a lot going on behind the scenes, but it is an incredible thing to observe and take part in.

14

WEDDING

Choose Your Own Adventure

I'm sure there are many of you reading this who are already married or are just not interested in weddings, which is totally understandable. I also know that a lot of people find me when they are looking for information about the K-1 fiance visa. And that is why I cannot pass up the opportunity to talk about weddings, because there are certainly an important population of you, who are very much immersed in this world right now. So if this doesn't apply to you, of course, you can skip this chapter, but there may be some tidbits here to glean about future celebrations, blending cultures, or even thinking about the wedding of a future child or even attending someone else's wedding.

To start with, when you're talking about a wedding, it is imperative to think about boundaries, first and foremost.

So if you are planning a wedding, especially when you and your partner are from different countries or cultures, you have a lot of traditions and expectations to manage. Perhaps one of you expects that it's going to be a multi-day celebration and one of you does not. Or maybe you have different feelings about how many people should be attending or who should be paying for it. There are many, many, many things to consider that may feel like they're working against you because your phone might be ringing off the hook from family members who are asking questions about the details that they are assuming are going to go their way.

You really need to sit down together, you and your partner, and talk about what your expectations and especially about what your non negotiables are. You may both have aspects of a wedding or celebration that are essential to you. And you will probably also have things that you don't feel that strongly about and you'd be willing to let go. But if all of these things are being treated like they're essential, then it's a lot of battles to be picking. It's a lot of hills to be willing to die on and potentially a lot of discord during what should be a beautiful time planning a beautiful celebration. So I would recommend talking together, just the two of you, first and foremost, about what is essential to you. What's meaningful to you? What's important to you? And what is it that you're not going to be interested in compromising about?

This might start with a bit of negotiation for the two of you. If you both have strong feelings, then you're going to need to figure those out before you go and introduce anyone else into the conversation. But once the two of you are on the same page, then you can open the floor up to a bit more input. Be careful how you do this initially at least, because if you position it in a way that makes parents, aunts, uncles, grandparents, and cousins think that you're looking for their input, you may get more than you bargained for. And you may get devoted family members who love you, but who think that you're actually asking them to plan this whole thing.

Now, of course, if it is what you're asking, there's nothing wrong with that. We had wedding celebrations that were both largely planned by others, and that was perfect for us in that time and the stress that we were under. But for others, that really might not be what they're looking for. So, know how much input you're open to, and don't bite off more than you can chew, as the saying goes. Ask for input about the things that you're willing to take input on, and be clear if there's something that you're not willing to take input on.

And then take all of that together and create something that's beautiful, that's meaningful to you, that incorporates and compromises. As an added benefit, along the way, you're having these conversations naturally with your loved ones about why it is that everything's not going just the way they want it to, why that's okay, and what it means to blend two cultures and two families. It doesn't mean that you have to take everything from both cultures. And it also doesn't mean that you can't take everything from both cultures. So the beautiful thing about blending multiple cultures is that you get to choose how you do it. There's no other family just like yours in the world. I mean, of course, there are absolutely other people with your two nationalities who are married to each other, but they're not you. No one's you. No one's going to do this just the way that you're doing it. So you can decide you're like the founding fathers/mothers/parents of your own little nation. You get to write your constitution or Declaration of Independence, to declare your autonomy and what your boundaries are around you and what it is that you're going to allow across your borders and what you're going to keep out on the other side.

A Note About K-1 Visa Weddings

Let's also touch briefly here on the K-1 process, as an extra aside for those who are currently in that process. Now I've made a lot of content about this already, but I'm going to basically summarize it here for you because you're already in the book and you don't need to dig out your phone or log on to your computer just to find the info. Here's my recommendation for the K-1 process, keeping in mind that I'm not a lawyer and I'm not a professional wedding planner. I've just done this myself and I have come alongside others while they're going through it.

So here's the thing: the K-1 visa gives you a 90-day window to marry your international fiance. In my mind, that does not mean that we should take the full 90 days and plan the perfect wedding. Now, that can be done, and I won't talk you out of it. But if you're looking for a way to preserve your sanity as much as possible and preserve your stress levels as much as possible, then what I think is the best way to do that is to separate your ceremony from your reception. So basically, that means getting married legally, as soon as possible so that you can continue the process with your adjustment of status and the next set of paperwork. After that, you'll be able to plan the celebration for a time when it's going to be better for you and more enjoyable and less stressful.

There are so many things causing stress in the life of a couple in the K-1 process. Likely, you are in a long distance relationship, though I would imagine some couples like my husband and I are able to be together in the other person's country and are only facing a few months apart. But many, many couples have been long distance for years and are now going through the uncertainty of hoping that there won't be any more distance and separation.

There's also financial pressure that comes once you're married as the non citizen partner won't be able to work until he or she is granted employment authorization, which may or may not come before his or her green card. Of course, there's also the stress of moving to a new country and potentially being around a new language. There are also family members to consider, especially if you are living under the same roof, which happens sometimes because when you're in a tight financial situation, moving in with family might feel like the best solution.

There are so many factors here to cause stress. We haven't even gotten into the expense of the immigration process, a new item on your budget at the same time that only one of you is authorized to work. There's just a lot to consider already. Wedding planning is a notoriously stressful time, and adding that into the mix might not be a recipe for peaceful coexistence and a stress-free life.

So what I would suggest or at least ask you to consider is to have a legal ceremony, whether that means going to the courthouse or having a friend perform a ceremony for you. Once the legality is taken care of, if you're still interested in having a bigger party at some point, then you can do that whenever you want. You can do it on the anniversary of your legal ceremony, you can do it a few months later, you can do it years later, or you can decide it's not important to you and never do it. This is really up to you in all the ways. You get to create this reality and there's nothing that's written in stone that says it has to be any one particular way or incorporate any particular traditions. As you're already in a place of blending cultures and picking the traditions that are meaningful to you, why not make it your own and do it in a way that's meaningful, stress free and memorable?

15

BOUNDARIES

As fun and sexy as boundaries are, they're essential in all of our relationships, with everyone, for the rest of our lives, as long as we all shall live. So you know, no pressure. It's not like it's that important. For the sake of this chapter, let's envision the different layers of boundaries as a series of concentric circles. We'll start at the outside and work our way in. The outermost ring is for work relationships. It's a great starting place because these are easier relationships to think about what boundaries are because you don't have the same attachments there that you might have, especially with family where it can get complicated. With family, we can have feelings of obligation and expectation that really complicate matters. So we're going to start with work, then we'll move into family and friends, and then your partner, and then yourself. That last one might sound bizarre and may have you wondering how you have boundaries with yourself. Don't worry about that yet — we'll get to it, and I'll do my darnedest to explain it in a way that makes sense.

Professional Boundaries

Let's begin with work. I'll start with a little story. I've had plenty of work environments where I've felt like, "Ah, these people are the best. They're my best friends. I love them so much. We're hanging out all the time and laughing together. And it's awesome. It's wonderful. I love it." But I think part of the reason why I appreciate that is because of work environments, where I realized that that just was not going to happen and I had to create boundaries. This happened really just in one job when I was teaching in South Korea. And it was the only time in my adult life when I've really felt, "Wow, my coworkers are really just my coworkers. And my friends are my friends. And there's no overlap here. It's just not happening." And it was kind of a strange thing, in the way it unfolded. I was the only foreign teacher in this rural school. And it was just the way things were set up that wasn't really ideal for having friendships formed there. I think part of that probably comes along with the territory of being an international teacher, especially if you're not as qualified as the local teachers are. Sure, I was working on my master's degree at the time, but all of my coworkers were certified teachers, established in the educational system of their country, the real deal. And then I come in to the picture, and I'm a native speaker, and I get all this respect and credibility just for that when really everyone else was doing so much hard work and I was just not a part of the system. So I want to be clear, I don't blame my coworkers and I wouldn't say they were unfriendly to me or anything like that. It's just that the system was not set up in such a way that we were ever really going to be all hanging out and going out for dinner and all that kind of stuff. And what happened in Korea, which was kind of a bizarre thing to me, was that, at least in the area where I was, every other person I knew who was a teacher, the staff at their schools would play volleyball together once a week. One of them mentioned this to me, which immediately gave me flashbacks to middle school gym class. I got sweaty just thinking about it, remember hell on earth, also known as middle school gym. As it turns out, it takes less than 5 hours a week to ruin every sport for the rest of someone's life. You know how it goes — you've met middle school aged children, or you were a middle school aged child, and you know what you were like at that age. But yes, if you take an awkward, dorky, gangly kid, and you put her on a team with all these kids who like to be sporty and very serious about it, that's just a recipe for disaster and for dreading that class every single day. So even as an adult in Korea, I knew that communal volleyball was a deal breaker for me.

That's when the boundary was created, and that's why I took it so seriously. If the communal activity had been anything but playing volleyball, I probably would have gone along with it. I can go for a hike or go out to dinner. But when it came to playing volleyball, I had to draw the line and set a boundary. And at that time, I was teaching in two different schools. And it happened that I was at the other school on the day that my main school played their regular volleyball game. Once, my co-teacher mentioned that the previous English teacher used to join the volleyball games, but there was no pressure or overt invitation for me to join. And it was natural in that moment to let the boundary remain where it was. I could see where my social life was and where my work life was, and I was comfortable with it. And, in some ways, by not having an overlap between my personal life and my professional life, it made it easier to relate at work, because things can get more complicated when there are personal relationships at stake. Now of course, I don't think this is essential in every work environment. But certainly we have those work environments where you can see what's going on or you can see that it is a potentially toxic environment, and you know that you want to set boundaries for your own comfort. Work is work, and life is life. Now as we move to the next ring of the diagram, it's a little more complicated.

Friends and Family

The next ring is for friends and family, though we will primarily focus on family. Friends certainly can overstep boundaries, but when we're talking about our romantic relationships, it's more likely our family that's going to be the complicating factor there. So there's an analogy that I heard from Glennon Doyle, where she was talking about her relationship being like an island. And to illustrate boundaries, she was saying that she and her partner get to decide who comes to visit the island. I love that image of an island out in the middle of the sea. It's not to say that others can't come hang out with us, but we get to decide because we control the harbor. Or we can think of it like a castle, and anyone who's not in the castle (or who isn't one of the two of us in this relationship) needs to ask permission to enter. If we're comfortable letting the drawbridge down, then we let the drawbridge down. And if we're not, then we don't, and there's probably a moat full of alligators if you don't respect our answer.

An example of an instance when this kind of interaction is common is when you're thinking about planning a wedding. These are the kinds of times where people in your family and your partner's family need to be aware of what your boundaries are, or else it's going to feel like they're storming the castle with their opinions of what you must do (or not do) at your wedding. They're knocking down the castle gate with opinions and traditions and assumptions, and you might be gasping for air as you try to get your voice heard. Maybe you already know what you definitely do or don't want to do at your wedding, or maybe there are some areas where you're open to input. But boundaries are like expectations, in the sense that if we don't communicate them, it's really unfair. If we have expectations for our partners, or for people in our lives, and we don't communicate those expectations to them but then we just get pissed off when they don't do the thing that we expect them to do, that's really unfair. It's like playing a mind game and expecting them to read your mind. It's like saying, "I'm fine," when you're not fine and wishing that they would figure out what the problem is without you needing to tell them. We know that's not fair, and we're all working on that, I'm sure. But in that same vein, if you have these boundaries and you don't make it clear where they are, then it becomes your responsibility, when people start overstepping them, to communicate, "This isn't okay, and I need you to take five steps back." The exception with this, of course, is if someone's overstepping boundaries in a way that's making you unsafe, then you need to make your safety your priority. In general, I promote being compassionate with how you express what your boundaries are to people. Instead of saying, "You should go away and never tell me your opinion ever again," you can offer compassion and say, "We're thinking of going in this direction, but here's an area where we'd like to have your help. But for this other thing, I think we've got that figured out." But, absolutely, the exception is that you don't have to be compassionate to somebody if they're endangering you or crossing physical boundaries that you're not comfortable with. For the concerns that aren't that serious, like flowers at your wedding, we can figure out ways to approach it from a place of compassion.

In the spirit of vulnerability, I'd like to share my own experience with boundaries in family. To start with, let me say that I think it's always a little challenging for adults to go back home after having moved out and lived on their own. For me, I've been an independent person since college and moving overseas, and yet when I go back to my parents' home, I can't help but feel like somewhat of a child again. If I stay with them for a week, or a month, or two years, which happened between college graduation and my first overseas job, I find myself almost asking permission to do things. It doesn't feel natural to treat the situation as if we're roommates, and instead I behave more like my child self, confirming with Mom and Dad that it's okay for me to go out and meet a friend. And this isn't something that they've demanded of me. If anything, I ask more so to confirm that they won't miss me too much and we won't have more fun hanging out by ourselves, anyway. Now, I think this happens to a lot of us, and to many of us it might not even feel like a problem. It didn't feel that way to me, and I've always really valued the close relationship that I have with my parents. But the thing is, when you get married, and you live in their home with your spouse, and then as time goes on, when you continue to spend time there with your spouse, you realize or maybe your partner realizes that this regression is happening, and that's where it can become a boundary issue. Because when I find myself in a place where my primary role in this interaction is as your child and not as another adult, then boundaries start getting crossed and it can quickly become obvious just how essential those boundaries were.

My example is as follows, and I won't go into too much detail since I wasn't the only person involved. My husband and I were spending a lot of time with my family, and we were also trying to figure out some things about our next trip to Turkey and the wedding that we would have there. And I think the way I broached the topic may have made it sound like I wasn't confident in my decision and that I was asking for input, where I really wasn't asking for it. But the point is that it made a member of my family feel like he needed to intervene and take over, which didn't go well, because he didn't do it in a nice way and someone got insulted. I found myself figuratively jumping in front of my husband to put a stop to that and to make it clear that we, the two of us and only the two of us, are a team. We are a unit, and you are a unit, and both of those units make decisions about their own lives. This isn't a democracy where we all have an equal vote. Rather, it is a democracy, but it's only the two of us in it. Your input is appreciated to a certain extent, but you're not making our decisions. And it was something that really has transformed our relationship with my family members, and everything is much better now. I'm no longer putting myself in that position where I'm making someone feel like they can tell me what to do. And it's something that in working through that I realized, this isn't about someone else being a jerk, this is about us putting ourselves in a position where that seemed like a necessary thing to do.

Since then, we've worked on rebuilding that relationship, which happens when hurtful things are said and people are offended. But that's how it works to create boundaries. It's like trying to hit a moving target. It doesn't just happen, and it takes readjustment until you get it just right. Something that you're comfortable sharing or discussing one day, you may not always be comfortable with sharing and discussing. And that's something that I think we have to be more understanding of with those people in our lives, because the same might be true for them. You know, when you establish a boundary with someone, they might realize you're doing that and respond in kind. Maybe they no longer feel comfortable sharing their feelings or their relationship details with you, and that's something that we learn to respect rather than being offended if someone's pulling away, if this is for their ultimate good and the best decision for their mental health, then who are we to say that they can't do that?

Boundaries with Your Partner

So the next layer in there is your partner. It's important to have protective boundaries around your relationship, but then you also need to have that protection around yourself too. This means in your relationship, you still have a boundary in there. You're together, you love each other, but you don't want to become codependent where someone else's happiness is your responsibility and you outsource responsibility for your happiness to that person. There's a quote from Rilke's "Letters to a Young Poet," and I think it's a great depiction of relationship and boundaries. He writes, "The love that consists in this, that two solitudes, protect and border and greet each other." And so the concept here in this that called out to me the first time I read it is that you have this solitude, like you are your own little universe, and you have your things that orbit around you and that you protect and you hold to yourself, and your partner has that too. And so there's the idea that love and loving someone is protecting their solitude from the world, but maybe from yourself too. This is saying, "We spend a lot of time together, I might be wanting some alone time, but you might be too and so even though I love you, even though I want to be with you all the time, well, maybe we should each be aware of protecting each other and our solitude and not merging so much together that we don't have that anymore and we lose ourselves in each other." I can be guilty of this when I want to watch a movie and I feel like I need my husband to join me. While he doesn't mind if I do that without him, it has felt to me in the past like it just has to be a shared activity. But I've come to realize that it's more important for him to be true to his desires than to always give in to mine, which is also what I would want him to understand about me. It's important to offer the same understanding to others that we so desperately crave for ourselves. So the idea, again, is to remember that if we are working on having boundaries and asking others to respect them, then also respecting it when our partner needs alone time is imperative. It's not about us, and it doesn't need to be taken personally. That's a great rule for life.

Boundaries of Self

So the last level to discuss here is self. And I just can't miss any opportunity to share this, because I think it's really an important message. When we talk about boundaries, it's clear that if there was a toxic person in your life who was rude and said unkind things to you, you would not hesitate to create boundaries there. You'd say, "That's really not cool. I need you to not talk to me that way. I don't appreciate it." And even if you wouldn't do that for yourself, if there was a toxic person in your life who was doing that to your partner, to a friend of yours, or to someone else that you love, you would create those boundaries. You'd know that this behavior is hurtful and harmful and that you don't need it in your life.

And yet, sometimes, we are that toxic person in our own heads. You might hear this little voice, and it sounds like your own voice, and when you make a mistake, it might say things to you like, " Gosh, you're so stupid. You're such an idiot. You always mess everything up. You don't deserve love. You're just a fool." That voice sucks when it talks to you like that. And if it's saying the kind of thing that we wouldn't accept from someone else, then why do we put up with it from ourselves? We accept it as normal, like that's just the way that we talk to ourselves. Well, that's not the way you talk to anyone else, I hope. And it's not the way you let anyone else talk to you, so I think it's really, really important to get to the bottom of it.

So here's my idea for how to set boundaries there. You can't really remove that part of your brain or build a fence in your head, but think of it that way. You can build a little fence in your mind. You can tell that voice, "This is what you're allowed to say to me, and these are things that you're not allowed to say to me." Once I understand that that voice isn't me, I can create boundaries from it. One thing that has worked wonders for me is changing the things that I say to myself by first becoming aware of these repeated tapes that play in my head. Let me give you an example. I noticed myself saying (silently, of course), "Gosh, I'm really struggling today." And this wasn't a rare occurrence, it was every day. If anything happened that was a little bit challenging, without even thinking about it, I'd say, "Wow, I'm really struggling." At some point, I started to notice it and disagree with it. I'd say, "No, I'm not. I might be tired, but I'm not struggling. Existence isn't pain, I'm fine." This voice was so dramatic, and I knew I wanted to change it. So I thought of ways to change the things I was saying to myself. I might say, "Wow, I worked really hard, so I'm feeling a little tired now." Or I could say, "Wow, I'm really growing." Growth can be hard and it can be painful, so why not replace "struggling" with "growing" until further notice? I could also say, "I'm proud of you. I'm proud of you for getting out of bed this morning." And of course it's important to do the same thing when you make a mistake, because that's normally when that voice gets to go to town on you. It might tell you all kinds of nasty things or bust out a potty mouth and really make you feel terrible about yourself. But we can silence it, and we can change it.

One great way to do this is to think about what you would say to a friend who made a mistake, since we are often so much more easily generous with people who are not ourselves. You might say, "It's okay. You'll do better next time." If your friend was feeling defeated about something, would you chime in and tell them, "You should feel bad because you're a loser and you didn't deserve something good in the first place"? I know you wouldn't do that, so now let's work on speaking that same way to ourselves. We can offer grace and kindness and understanding to ourselves, too.

Special K-1 Considerations

Going through an immigration process or reuniting from being long distance is one of those great opportunities to bump into each other and have awkward conversations and figure out what works. I don't look back at those early K-1 days with my husband like, "Wow, those were the best times of our relationship," by any stretch because so much about that time was difficult. But when I look at where we are now, I remember that where we are now is the direct result of what happened then. Both of us went on major journeys of personal growth, and it's hard, of course, to have intense conversations about expectations and feelings and all of that kind of stuff. But it can bring you together in a way that shocks you in the best possible way. So my advice is to go into this time with the expectation for yourself that there are parts of this that will be stressful and there are parts of it, that will be beautiful, but it's such a catalyst for growth. What a great way to start relationship, by growing together, doing all that hard growing work, establishing your roots, so that in the future you get to reap the benefits of leaves, flowers, fruits, and all of that good, beautiful stuff.

There was one episode of the Borderless Stories podcast with Naira Bonilla of the Amor Diverso podcast where we talked about boundaries, though we didn't really call them that. She shared about her relationship, which went from long distance to living together and then back to long distance. My first thought when we were talking about that was how hard it would be not to become codependent when you are together. Knowing that it's going to be taken away from you again in the future, or knowing how much you've missed spending time together, it's so natural to want to be together all the time, every waking minute. We often learn where boundaries need to exist by messing them up or by crossing them, so it makes sense that we might overdo it on the togetherness and then, with time, realize that we need to establish time and space for solitude. That's when it's important to ask the question together of what you want your relationship to look like and what you can do or change to make that a reality.

We almost need to set conversational boundaries with our partners, especially at the end of the workday. Even if you're not living together at this point or if you're still long distance, it's worth thinking about what your reality will be when you are living under the same roof. At the end of a workday, how you start interaction together when you're in the same room again is crucial. Let me explain this with my own example of how I've messed this up in the past. Let's say one of you works from home and one of you is out, working with a bunch of preschoolers, which we can all agree is tiring. When the preschool teacher comes home, if the other partner greets him or her with, "Hey, let me tell you everything I did today. I'm so excited about all these things. Isn't this great?" as hard as it may be to believe, the exhausted preschool teacher may not be that receptive to this. Instead, the other partner could try asking, "How are you? How was your day? Are you ready for me to tell you about my day? Or should I maybe wait until you've like taken off your shoes and sat down? And maybe had a snack?" By asking those questions, you are checking in and asking if the other person is ready to meet you at your level. If not, then you know and you can put a pin in that thought until he or she is ready to connect.

When you're in the K-1 process, that will be your reality for a while. You'll come home and your partner will be at home waiting because, as you know, he or she won't be able to work yet. And so you are going to need to have a conversation about how that transition time is going to go. You can establish that boundary or expectation for what that transition time will look like. Instead of coming home and snapping out of frustration, "Can you just be quiet for five minutes?!" you can talk about it. You can say, "Hey, I'm probably going to need about 10 minutes [or 30 minutes or four hours, you know yourself better than I do] to decompress before I'm going to be human again. So I'm just gonna stop being a human for a little while, and I'll be right back with you when the transition is complete."

16

IN-LAWS

In-law relationships are notoriously complicated. There's a reason this is a meme in our American culture where we talk about mothers-in-law and in laws visiting as if it's universally understood that this is a challenging or bad or complicated thing. Now I think it's really important to be clear that there is no such thing as one side of our family being good and the other side being bad. I know this is a trope that plays out a lot where we like visiting one side of the family and we don't like visiting the other side. It's important to acknowledge though that even if one side of your family, either yours or your partner's, was hurtful or challenging in the past and maybe even in the present, that the experience has shaped you or your partner into the person that you are today. So it's important not to demonize one side of the family.

Now, navigating in-law relationships is ultimately going to come down to boundaries as well. So it requires, for one thing, becoming aware of boundaries with your own parents, grandparents, aunts, uncles, siblings, and so on, because if you expect these boundaries to exist with your partner's family, but you don't instate them with your own family, then that's a double standard and that's not cool. So with your own family, this means establishing yourselves as adults and as equals. The nature of your relationship has to shift from being a dependent child to being an independent adult. The same thing will have to happen of course with the other side of the family. But here's the thing: we can run into challenges and issues with this because it might feel more natural to have these boundaries if we're dealing with the side of the family that might be more focused on individuality. So some cultures are more inclined that way. For the way I was raised in the US, I wasn't really raised with a sense of obligation to family and to the greater community around me. It was more about doing the best for myself. And of course there are other cultures in the world where that sense of familial connection and community tie is so strong that that's the priority and people may have expectations put on them from a very young age to adhere to the needs of those around them. It's important to be very, very clear that neither one of these is better than the other. These are just different. So I can't say, "Well just because I was raised to value my independence and my individuality that's the only way to go and that's 100% the best thing."

I know that there are things that happen and there are people that fall through the cracks of society because it feels like no one's looking out for them. And I think there's a lot of unfortunate stuff that comes from only looking at ourselves. At the same time, I don't think ignoring or denying ourselves to focus on others is always the best way either. So in this section, in this whole book, I have no desire to cast any aspersions on different ways of valuing individuals or family. Regardless, the conflict can arise if one of you is from a more family oriented culture and one of you is from a more individual oriented culture. Then setting these boundaries with your families or with the in-laws might feel more natural in one case than in the other. For example, in my family, it became necessary to set boundaries at some point and that wasn't that big of a challenge for my family to accept because they had done the same thing with their own families.

But then when we look at doing similar things, for example with my husband's family, you're not going to have the same kinds of conversations because there just is more togetherness. It's more natural for us to spend time together when we were together than to isolate ourselves or go off and do our own thing. Now that has become our reality that we do do our own thing and we do create that space and that boundary, but that's happened as a result of my husband and I working through it together and he and I discussing it and it had to be something that he valued too. So what that means and how to get there is to have that conversation with your partner about what your needs are. If you're going to spend time in this family culture, immersed with family and you aren't okay with doing that 100% of the time, then you need to communicate clearly with your partner what you need to do to take care of yourself. This is of course, a time when it's really important to be careful about how you speak and to tread lightly, not to go into a conversation saying, "Hey, I don't want to spend that much time with your parents." That's hurtful, especially when you've been apart. That's really not something that people generally want to hear. But if you can go into it and say, "You know, I've realized how much I need time alone or one on one time with you in order to really feel like my bucket is full. So do you think it's possible for us to make some time for that to happen?" Then you're posing this as a thing that's about you and that you're hoping that this person is going to be able to help you fix. You're putting the onus on yourself and then inviting your partner to join you in solving that conundrum is much, much better than lashing out or protesting.

Then this can be a much more natural way for things to evolve, by your partner then taking the lead on that and saying, "Okay, yeah, maybe we don't have to do all the things together all the time." So in both of our cases with my family and then also with my husband's family, it was important for the one of us who was the child to be the one in the driver's seat in establishing these boundaries.

If there's a conflict, like in my case, when there was a conflict in my family, even though my husband was affected by things that happened in that conflict, it wasn't on him to decide what our appropriate boundaries were. It had to be on me. It was my job to figure out what needed to change because I had to take responsibility for that. If he had taken responsibility for it, then I could have ultimately ended up blaming him and saying, it's your fault that I don't get to be close in the same way that I was in the past. But by me being in the driver's seat and saying, "Okay, I see where I've created this reality, I don't like what it is, so I want to change it." That's gotten us to a place that feels a lot better and a lot healthier.

And the same thing has happened with his family

where when we take space that's got to be on him to decide how much time we need to spend together and how much time we can spend apart. If I come in and I'm saying, "I'm deciding and we're doing this or we're not doing that," then I could become a source of resentment, because that's not really my place.

I think it's important for partners to be champions for their in-laws. So what I mean by that is if a conflict comes up between a child and his or her parents, so between you and your parents or between your partner and his or her parents, then it's a very, very good thing if the spouse is championing the parents and reminding their child of what's so great about them. It can feel tempting if there's a conflict and your partner's upset with their family, maybe you know, your life would be easier if you only had one set of grandparents to worry about, so maybe you might feel tempted to say, "Sure, we don't need to see them anymore." And in rare, rare situations, that may be the answer. In the case of abuse and manipulation, certainly, I'm not going to tell you that you must mend fences. But outside of those extreme cases, the majority of the time, the things that come up that cause these sorts of conflicts aren't worth severing relationships over. So as the spouse jumping on that and trying to say, "Hey, yeah, let's erase them from the family tree," is not something that you're probably going to feel great about in the long run. Many of us, at the ends of our lives or later on in our lives, we regret the relationships that we've let fall apart. So if when your partner is in a volatile situation with their family, feeling upset, feeling like withdrawing, it's a really, really wonderful thing if you can listen, can respond respectfully, and can remind him or her of who you know that they really are. We aren't all our best when we're in conflict, so maybe if things are said that are hurtful, they're not meant, but they've still been said. And you can help remind your partner of the truth, asking, "Well, who do they show us to be the rest of the time?"

The reality is, when two or more people are upset with each other, and then another person jumps in and says, "Yeah, hey, those guys suck!" then when things are repaired, ultimately in the future, you find yourself saying, "Well now I wish I hadn't said that. That was uncomfortable or that was hurtful or that it was unnecessary." It's better to avoid saying it in the first place and to take on the role peacemaker. And you can do that for each other. You and your partner can mutually agree that, first and foremost, both of your families are loved and valued. They both have important roles in your lives. One is not better than the other. One is not more important than the other. And now what are the boundaries that we want to have with them? How much do we want to have them influence our lives? How much do we want to share with them and how is this relationship going to work now as adult families navigating that relationship?

17

THE IMPORTANCE OF COMMUNITY

We're concluding our time together with the idea, "They wouldn't understand," and the need to find community. I'm going to explain first what I mean by, "They wouldn't understand," explain why I think community for people in these kinds of relationships is important, tell a little bit of my own story of my journey from being a lone wolf to being someone who's kind of addicted to community (in a good way), and finally closing with some practical tips and advice for finding your people.

"They Wouldn't Understand"

The idea behind everything that I've created here at

Borderless Stories has been creating what I wish had existed in the earlier stages of my own relationship. There have been a number of times when I found myself turning to my search bar and looking for a community or looking for some kind of resources to help us through immigration or just wondering if there was anybody else out there going through the same thing. It was, at times, kind of hard to come by that. And you can feel like there's something wrong with you when nobody around you can relate to what it is that you're going through. What I realized is that many people who were already in my life prior to me meeting my husband couldn't relate to the challenges and the disagreements that he and I were having because they weren't in a relationship of the same nature.

Every relationship has conflicts, of course, but when the nature of the conflict is a cultural difference, sometimes other people can almost be intolerant of it because we can so deeply feel that something is absolutely right or is absolutely wrong. It can be really hard to be open minded enough to say, "Well maybe someone has a different cultural background and so they feel differently about gender roles," for example. Gender roles are the thing that comes up the most, even though they weren't a major issue in my relationship, they are something that people tend to say, "This is the right way, my way or the highway." And while I understand that, of course, and I'm totally pro-women and know women can do absolutely anything and everything that they want to do, we still have to acknowledge that in a different culture, someone might have been exposed to a different way of thinking. It doesn't mean that they will persist in thinking that way, but it's part of their cultural makeup. It's a portion of the part of their cultural iceberg, which is deep, deep underwater, and so it affects them whether they want it to or not. And it's only when we start to investigate ourselves and explore and try to work through those things and figure out why we feel the way that we do that we're able to move past that.

I first noted that I wasn't going to want to share my experiences with people in my life through a few ways that people had approached me in conversation that made me think, "When I'm in that situation, I might not want to share." I've had people in my life question if I would ever be able to "settle down" because I was so independent as a young woman. That made me realize, "Wow, you don't think that I can do this maybe or it's going to be hard for me or the way that I'm going through the world, the things that I'm doing, the choices that I'm making aren't relatable to you so you can't imagine that someone like me can embark on a relationship like this." Many things that people said about what marriage was like surprised me from a young age. It was often the recurring idea, "Oh, you'll understand this when you're married, you'll understand why we don't want to see our friends and why we just want to be together. You'll understand [XYZ] thing once you're married." This painted a picture for me of what people thought marriage was. And I remember at a tender, young age when someone said, "You'll understand when you're married why we don't want to hang out with our friends anymore," I remember thinking, "I don't ever want to get married if that's the way that it is, if it's going to make me not want to have friends anymore." Granted, things of course do change once you get married, but I've always been of the belief that it's up to me and my partner what changes, and it's not up to what anyone else tells us is going to change.

People show their feelings about what something is through the way that they communicate about it and that helped me realize this might not be the place where I come and say, "Hey, my boyfriend and I are trying to figure out how to balance who does what chores around the house" or something like that. I can see that being the kind of thing that someone would have absolute opinions about, whether that's, "You should do them because you're a woman," which I don't think anyone would have said to me or, "You should split them absolutely evenly" or, "He should do everything" or whatever it would be. I just didn't see it being something that we could have an open, honest dialogue about.

People who love you dearly are looking out for you most of the time. And when they're looking out for you, they want to protect you from harm. They want to prevent you from getting hurt, and they want to make sure that you're safe. At times this means that if you're coming to them with a problem, it could be perceived as a threat to your comfort or to your safety, and they might just say, "Hey, get out of there." If you come to somebody that you love and you say, "My boyfriend and I had a silly argument about _____," they might say, "Dump him!" It's entirely within the realm of possibility that somebody would tell you that. And it's not that they don't love that person; it's that they love you so much that they want to make sure you're safe and you're okay and they don't know how it's going to be for you to navigate through that challenge. They want to protect you and keep you safe, so the instinct is to get rid of the threat. To them, the threat is this person who doesn't see the world the same way that you do because that can be scary to someone else.

That doesn't mean that there aren't people that you can share with. You might feel like there are things that you can't say out loud to somebody because they're going to judge you. But I want you to know that there are people out there who you can share with. You can talk about your immigration journeys, for example, and they're not going to judge. Immigration is another thing that many people from the outside might look at and say, "Oh wow, you had a practical conversation about whether you should get married or not. Hmm. Sounds to me like that's not very romantic. Are you sure that this person's not using you for a visa?" These are real comments that I'm sure some of you reading this have had said or suggested to you. The reality of that, of course, is that marriage is a practical decision. And for anyone who decides to get married, you have to talk about things. You have to talk about logistics and if you want it to work, you've got to know that you have a plan. If you're from the same country, that might just mean saying, "Should we move into your apartment or mine?" Oh my gosh, that's not a romantic conversation to have. You should dump that person! Maybe they're just using you for your great apartment! No, it's just that we don't want to have two apartments; we want to live together, so where should we live? But if you're from different countries and are trying to decide how to be together and which country it might be easier for you both to live in, that's a practical conversation that has to happen. It doesn't mean that romance is dead and you don't love each other. It just means that you're trying to prepare yourselves for success and not end up separated by an ocean. So there are safe places where you can share that kind of story. There are people who are safe people for you to say that to, who aren't just going to say, "Hmm, that sounds sketchy to me. It sounds like that's not real. That doesn't sound very romantic."

My Story

I've said this before, and I'm sure I will say it again, but it's important enough that I feel good about repeating myself. The purpose of Borderless Stories, of the community that I've created, of this book, of all of our resources, is never, ever, ever to say, "It's so hard to love someone from a different country. They are so difficult. They are so challenging. We need each other because it's a challenge." That's never, ever a message that I want to send and I try to be very clear about that. What brings us together is not complaining about our partners and saying, "You'll never believe what he or she did today. This is just unacceptable." Rather, it's that this is a journey for all of us of personal growth, of exploration, of learning, and of discovery. There are so many things that get uncovered, at least in my experience, as you go through a relationship like this.

Wanting to have a safe space where we can come and share those things, I never want it to be the kind of place where someone would come and say, "Based on my experience with this one person from this country who I happen to be married to, I'm going to make sweeping generalizations about that whole country or their entire religion or people of their race" or any of those kinds of things. It's never that. It's never going to be a place where I say, "Let's have a conversation thread just about what we don't like about all these different nationalities." Not even a little bit. We all have different stories. We are from different places, our partners are from different places, and we're not cookie cutter mirror images of each other, but we're all on this journey of discovery. We all have to ask ourselves the same kinds of questions, like where are we going to live? How can I learn more about myself so I can better understand this person that I'm in a relationship with? How are we going to blend cultures when it comes time to raising children? How are we going to deal with language in that situation?

Whatever our challenges may be, our partners are not hard to love. Their being from a different country does not make them hard to love. It doesn't make them "exotic" either. In the early stages of my own international journey, I lost track of the number of times I heard, "Oh you're going to meet someone in this country or in that country or whatever."

At the time, it was always frustrating to me to hear that, because that was never, ever, ever my intention or goal of each subsequent move. I shot it down every single time someone said it. "This isn't one big mission to just take home a souvenir of a person who doesn't have their own identity and their own life and their own value and all that stuff. I just want someone to come be a part of my story." One funny example of this was when I was really excited about going to Turkey after that job opportunity materialized when I was least expecting it. I was talking with someone who was excited for me, which was great because there were people certainly who weren't that excited and were much more concerned about my safety. Now we were talking about that part of the world that a lot of people do tend to ask questions about safety, and

I hadn't gotten any of those questions when I left for Ireland or Germany. So, this person was talking to me and was saying, "Oh, Turkey, you know, they have those great olive–" and I immediately starting nodding along as she says the word "olive" because I'm thinking, "Why yes, I do love olives! I know they grow olives in Turkey. I'm going to have great olives, great olive oil, just all the olive things." But then she actually finished her sentence and it wasn't "olives" but "olive-skinned men." That was a record scratch moment for me. "Whoa, wait, timeout. No, no, no, no. That's not what this is. That's not what this is for me. This is a job. This is a beautiful region in a beautiful country and olives? Heck yes. Sign me up."

I wasn't comfortable with the idea of meeting an "exotic" person, and I don't see the fact that I met my husband as fulfillment of that prophecy. We were just two humans, two souls who connected, and decided to make a go of it together. Side note, if I ever start talking about this person that I love more than anyone else like he's just an exotic accessory in my life, please feel free to give me a reality check.

With all that said, let's move from the lone wolf version of me I was at the time of that story to the person I am today who counts community in her core values. If you had told me five years ago that I'd be saying that, I would never have believed you. I think many people at some point in their lives have a negative experience with community, whether that's middle school mean girls or some kind of toxic experience in an organization or place of work. It can be really easy after that to feel like community is not for you. I had an experience like that in college with a group that I thought was really wonderful and then ended up being really toxic and really hurtful and I didn't realize for a long time the true implications of that and how much that really made me withdraw into my shell like a turtle or a crab. Following that, my experience living in different places certainly was a journey of discovery for me, sure, but there was also an amount of being aware that if I'm only committed to being someplace for a year, then you probably don't really expect me to be in true community with you. At the end of this commitment, I can remove myself from it and say, "Well, it's been great knowing you. I'll try to stay in touch, but I also know I'm not that great at staying in touch, so have a good life." And, to an extent, that's exactly what happened at the end of contracts or upon deciding to leave a place. A lot of relationships have fallen by the wayside because that's the nature of what happens when you live thousands of miles away from people.

So, while travel can seem adventurous and it can seem like a great way to go and connect with people, when it's long-term travel and you're committed to being in a place for months or years, it's really easy to still have your own safe space. So you can be like me and you can be an introvert who lives in a different country and does things there, sure, but sometimes still spends a whole day just in your own apartment or in your own hostel, just doing your own thing. It was in Turkey, because of friendships there and obviously also meeting Hüseyin, my husband, where for the first time in a long time, I had that community feeling again. We were all invested in each other, not just he and I, but our group of friends as well. Starting to have that feeling like we were creating our own family, where we spent holidays together and shared life together, was a nice foray back into that environment.

Despite that, moving back to the States I found I had been gone for so long and felt so disconnected from community that it was still easy to want to retreat and to be so invested in building our relationship that I didn't want to pour a lot of energy into something else or someone else. Plus, I didn't know how grown-ups make friends anyway. I'm not a member of any groups that are automatically going to have friendships attached to them, and I've only ever really made friends at work or at school. Working from home and relying on the Internet was new territory, and I was so unsure of myself. So it's an interesting phenomenon that creating community has become such a part of what I do because it's not something I would have guessed. If you look at a shy seven-year-old whose face turns bright red when someone asks her a question, you wouldn't imagine that decades down the road that kid is going to be sending emails to strangers on the Internet and saying, "Hey, be my friend, let's talk about deep things!"

What I would say about community is that doing life with other people and bumping into other people has been one of the most valuable and best decisions that I've ever made. This is true not just in things that I've created but in communities that I've taken a chance and been brave and said, "I'm going to go be a part of this and I'm going to try being myself." That's a challenge I think a lot of us face, like is this a safe space for me to be me? If I share, am I going to get hurt or if I share, is it going to be wonderful and amazing? And it's really important to make sure that you're sharing in a safe space. Brené Brown is one of my absolute favorite writers and speakers, and she talks about vulnerability and the need for boundaries. Not everybody has earned your vulnerability, and it has to happen within boundaries. You don't want to go up to the teller at the bank and tell them about your relationship with your father. Just because someone asks how you are doesn't mean you need to get into all the nitty gritty details. Sharing should be a reciprocal kind of thing, not that we need to keep score in our relationships, but that we can know that someone is a safe person to share with because they also share with us. That builds faith and trust that our secrets are safe with our confidants.

Find Your Folks

Then there's nothing left to do but learn where to find your people. I know the Internet loves to tell us, "Your vibe attracts your tribe," but many of us are steering away from that because we've realized that using the word "tribe" in that way can be very offensive to people who are members of tribes and for whom that word has a deeper meaning for than just a friend group. It's not language that I want to use with my community and I don't want to appropriate that. So, I sat down with a rhyming dictionary one day and explored what else we can say. I love that that saying rhymes, but I certainly don't want to use the same words. The best I could come up with is, "Your jokes attract your folks." This is the first time I've shared that in writing, but it's something that helps me remember to be authentically myself. I know I can have a little bit of a wacky sense of humor and if you listen to me talk at all you'll likely notice facial expressions, tones, and references that may not come across as professional in the classical meaning of the word. But that's what it comes down to for me. It might be different for somebody else, but for me, if I can't express my sense of humor and if I don't feel safe to do that, then it's not a community that I'm going to mesh in.

If I'm with potential friends and I'm really trying to keep it all together and not say anything that might be perceived as strange or do anything odd with my face, that's going to be exhausting for me. That's my introvertedness rearing its head and saying, "If you can't do that stuff, that releases tension and energy and it energizes you, then it's not for me." So this is my way of saying be yourself and trust that your people are there. Your jokes attract your folks, whether your jokes are knock knock jokes or just the way that you move through the world. Even if you don't like jokes, the things that you laugh at, whatever that is will help you connect with your people. In life it's important to be able to laugh at things and to be able to have fun and not take it all too seriously. So find your folks, and use your jokes. Your jokes will help you find your folks.

Here's my advice for how to find your people. Contrary to what you might be thinking, this is not a sales pitch for why you should come and join my community. By no means is that what this is because there are billions of people on the planet. They do not all belong in my community because they're not all folks who are going to be attracted to my jokes. That's the reality, and I accept that. I welcome that because trust me, when I say I do not want ever to have 7 billion people focusing their eyes and their attention on me, that's not for me. But here are my suggestions for how you can find your people, and it's not just by telling knock knock jokes.

Take a step

The first thing is to take a step, any step. I have in the past been someone who has been paralyzed by inaction because I wanted to take the right step. There was a time in my life when, if I had two choices, I wouldn't know what to do. I'm not even talking about big, monumental choices. It was just any time that I had choices to make, I wanted to know that I was choosing the right one. Maybe I would need to meditate about it or journal about it or take some action to help me be sure that it was the right choice. A big shift for me came when I realized I needed forward momentum. It was easier to redirect once I was already moving than to start from a stop and go anywhere. I can steer this thing, but when I stop it, it takes a lot more energy to get it moving again. So that said, taking the first step to initiate something, anything. The first time that I organized my annual virtual retreat, it started with one simple step. While I was preparing to meet a brand new Internet friend (Neha O'Rourke), the idea occurred to me that some kind of virtual summit or retreat would be a really cool thing to organize. Rather than keeping it to myself because I wasn't sure how it would all unfold, I just decided to say it. Put it out there and get some feedback. She was so supportive and encouraging and the rest is history — just a few months later, our first Love + Culture Haven kicked off with over 20 speakers, and it's only growing and improving from there.

But I had to take that first step and if I hadn't taken a step, nothing else would have happened. And things really did fall into place. The right tools that we needed to make it happen found their way into my possession, whether that was the universe bringing it to me or

Internet ads doing their job. If I hadn't said that thing out loud, and if I hadn't reached out to Neha in the first place, none of it would have happened.

Don't lurk

That's a natural transition into our second piece of advice: don't lurk. This is something a lot of us do, especially when we're hanging out on social media — for me, that's on Instagram. That's the place where I feel this happens the most and we just lurk, watching stories, clicking, scrolling, swiping. It's really easy to lurk and it's really easy to not connect and to feel like we're connected because we're watching someone or we're hearing their voice. We feel like we know them, but we don't because they don't know us. Relationship goes both ways. I listen to podcasts and sometimes I feel like the hosts are my friends because I hear their voices so much, but of course, they don't have a clue who I am. I am not even a blip on the radar because I'm just one in a sea of many, many people who are hearing them and because they're doing their jobs well I feel connected to them. We might have that on a much smaller scale, not just with famous people or people who have massive audiences, but even with people who we've found on social media because they seem cool, so we follow them. We watch their stories and we feel like we're friends, but no real connection has happened. So take a first step and leave a comment on a picture that they post or reply to their story. I don't know why we don't do that, but maybe we feel like it's annoying to the other person. But it's not. If somebody responds to something I share and they relate to it and they share a story of their own, if they take the effort to do that, I always, always, always appreciate it. When someone who has the potential to be a peer or a friend makes a connection, it's just the best. So, resist the call to lurk. Overcome the urge to delay or make excuses; just do it. If there's someone in your life who you feel might understand what you're going through, and they might be able to be a friend, what's the worst that could happen? They don't respond to your message? Okay, great, try again with somebody else. There are plenty of people out there that you can connect with and that you can become friends with, and all it takes is one action.

It doesn't have to take a long time or a lot of effort. Relationships can really grow and blossom and bloom faster than you might realize. A lot of the people who spoke at the first virtual retreat I didn't know a month prior to it, and because of that experience that we shared, they all became really special to me. They gave me (and our community) so much and we connected and we shared really deep things and it felt great.

Technology isn't evil

The final piece of advice here is remember that technology isn't evil. Social media isn't evil. These are tools that can be used for good or bad, just like money. Money is a tool: you can use it to send someone to college or you can use it to hire a hit man. It's what you do with it that determines whether it is good or bad. The same thing is true with social media and technology. You can use it to waste time and to make yourself feel bad when you're comparing yourself to people, or you can use it to connect with some of the most wonderful people that you'll ever meet. I'm a firm believer in that; every single person who participated in our first retreat, apart from my husband, was someone that I met on social media, without fail. So all that to say, use it for good. If you're feeling isolated, if you're feeling alone, reach out. Your phone is probably in your hand already, just use it to make that effort and to take that first step. You never, never know what might happen.

And if you're reading this and you do want to be a part of our community, then yes, of course we'd love to have you. You're so welcome and you know how to find me (check out our website, if you don't already know that).

I hope this has been helpful to you. I'm so grateful for your time and your presence and your energy and I wish you all the best with your life, with your love, and with your days to come.

ACKNOWLEDGEMENTS

Without the motivational, emotional, grammatical, and financial support of so many dear people listed here, none of this would have been possible.

To Hüseyin, I mean, obviously thank you for starting a new adventure together once upon a time or else not one single word in these pages would have been written. Thank you for exceeding my expectations of who I needed, wanted, or deserved to be with, and thank you for being my love, partner, teacher, and friend.

To Jane and Mike McCormick, thank you for continuing to breathe life into me. Thank you for offering support and encouragement, even when your parent radar is surely shrieking that a stable job might be a safer bet. You truly embody the adage of parents giving their children roots and wings, and I am so grateful to you.

To Mary McCormick, Bob and Linda Nachtrieb, Mark and Rebecca Nachtrieb, Karen and Dan Hayes, and John and Bev Nachtrieb, it's an honor to get to learn from all of you. You've all played such important parts in this journey, from your generosity to your asking of good questions to simply being who I want to be when I grow up.

It only follows that after acknowledging my own wealth of aunts and uncles, it's time to thank the folks who made me an aunt myself. To John, Rachel, Audrey, Greg, Eliana, Lewis, and Rose McCormick, it's been the most fun being with you all. Thank you for so many reasons to smile, for bottomless kombucha, and for accidentally giving me cat food for Christmas.

To my Turkey family, thank you for sharing your most precious son with me, for your bravery to love across an ocean, and for loving me through and despite my inadequate Turkish skills. It won't always be like this, I promise.

To Mary Nachtrieb, the first set of eyes to read my complete first draft, I am so grateful for your friendship, rekindled in a few transformative summer days. Thank you for your sharp eye, generous feedback, and an introvert's appreciation for Zoom call frequency.

To the coaches that I worked with the year this book baby was gestating, Maggie Giele, Cassandra Le, and Andrea Valeria, thank you for pushing when I needed to be pushed and being generous with your ideas but never giving me the answers.

To my accountability partners and business besties, Viktoria Undesser and Carol Perez, thank you for being my rising tide and always being up for a laugh even when it feels like everything is falling apart. We have a unique gift for taking turns being butt kickers and hot messes, and I don't take any of it for granted.

To my early readers, Neha O'Rourke, Lena Papadopoulos, Camilla Quintana, Elizabeth Mariyo, and Mariam Ottimofiore, thank you for your friendship. It's a vulnerable position to be in, sharing your heart in written form, but I never doubted that you were a safe space to do just that.

To all of the women I've met through Borderless

Stories, Love + Culture Haven, and the wonders of the internet: you really do make the world go round. Thank you for taking up your unique space in this world and for doing it so darn well.

To Holly and Carrie, thank you for taking a chance on me and opting into what has undeniably become one heck of a sweet little community. It's been a joy to follow along on both of your journeys.

To Lisa and Daniel Tubbs, thank you (respectively) for being one of my oldest friends and one of my newest. Without the two of you, this book and a poorly-made audiobook counterpart would be launched into the world with exactly zero fanfare. Your generosity is an inspiration.

To Candell Graff, thank you for years of laughs and memories and for being equally afraid of everything with me in college. Your support does not go unnoticed, and it makes me wonder if you missed your calling as a cheerleader and feel darn lucky to be your friend.

To Sarah Daniel, our friend and surrogate daughter, thank you for being the best surprise souvenir from a job I never intended to have. Your friendship is a delight.

Thank you to Joanne Ladio, Judy Gentz, and Ty Melgren for your unexpected but much-appreciated generosity. 'Tis a gift to know you all.

Finally, thank *you*, dear reader, for sticking with me this long. I may be the only one who considers a book incomplete unless I've read every single acknowledgement, but if you're still here then maybe that's not the case. I hope this book has been helpful to you, and I can't wait to get to know you.

ABOUT THE AUTHOR

KC McCormick Çiftçi is the founder of Borderless Stories, where she provides coaching for people in intercultural relationships, leads a membership community, and hosts a podcast about loving across borders. Borderless Stories was created when KC and her Turkish husband were beginning the K-1 fiance visa process while navigating an intercultural, international relationship. Connect with her at www.BorderlessStories.com to keep in touch.